Wild Wild Walton

ALSO BY RONNIE MCBRAYER

But God Meant It for Good

Keeping the Faith: Passages, Proverbs, and Parables

Leaving Religion, Following Jesus

Keeping the Faith, Volume 2

The Jesus Tribe

Esther

How Far Is Heaven?

The Gospel According to Waffle House

Fruits of the Cotton Patch

Wild Wild Walton

Ronnie McBrayer

DEDICATION:

This book is dedicated to the memory of the Walton County Sheriffs and Deputies killed in the line of duty and to their families.

Published by Bird on a Wire Media.

LAYOUT, DESIGN AND CREATIVE: Tim Ryals. All original art work, cover design and book layout is copyrighted by Tim Ryals, © 2015. All rights reserved. Its use is prohibited unless prior written permission from the artist is obtained.

HISTORICAL PHOTOS: State Archives of Florida, Florida Memory, www.floridamemory.com

ISBN-13: 978-0692471586
ISBN-10: 0692471588

ACKNOWLEDGEMENT

The stories contained within this book are historically based in the folklore tradition. As such, elements of fact, oral story-telling, and narration are combined to create a genre unique to itself. This work was inspired and largely based on the 2015 Grit & Grace production, "Wild, Wild Walton." Where applicable, those stories are used by Grit & Grace's express permission.

Grit & Grace is the Official Folk Life Production of Walton County; a non-profit community-based theater group whose mission and purpose is to preserve the history of Walton County, Florida through storytelling, music, and dance based on the stories and legends of Walton County.

The Official Folk Life Production
of Walton County, Florida

Post Office Box 62, DeFuniak Springs, Florida 32435 www.gritandgrace.org

i

CONTENTS

FOREWORD

by SHERIFF MICHAEL A. ADKINSON, JR.

It is with great pleasure that I recommend
to you this book that covers such an important
and challenging time in Walton County's
history. Indeed, in the "pioneer days" of the
Florida Panhandle, there was often a lack of
both law and order. County borders stretched
far and wide, and travel was most difficult.
This made our woods and bayous welcoming
habitats for the criminal element. Yet, in the
tradition of the Wild West lawman, courageous
men and women put on the badge to reverse this
course of events.

Officially, law enforcement
history began in Walton County
when Michael Vaughn (left) was
appointed the first sheriff in
1827 by Governor Duval. Florida
wasn't even a state then. It
was a United States territory
recently acquired from Spain. Law enforcement
during this period, and for many decades to
come, was solely reactionary, not preemptive.
There were not the resources or staff to
prevent crime, only to respond once a crime
had been committed. Consequently, as several
of the stories in this book show, the people of
the community were responsible for policing

themselves, so to speak. The results were not always favorable toward justice.

Along with Sheriff Vaughn, at the time of this writing, 42 people have held the Office of Sheriff of Walton County. You'll meet a few of these folks, or see reference made to them, as you read: Sheriffs Neil McPherson Campbell (1873-1877); William Bethune McLeod (1878-1879); James Murdock Bell (1909-1916) and his brother, Thaddeus "Thad" Bell (1917-1933). The Bell brothers both died in office or shortly after leaving the position; James from cancer and Thad from complications after a severe gunshot wound.

Sadly, Bell was not the only Walton County Sheriff or deputy to be wounded in the line of duty. Deputy Thomas G. Blount was shot and killed while exercising a warrant, August 16-17, 1929. His great-granddaughter, Lieutenant Angie King Hogeboom, proudly followed in his footsteps, and today is with the Walton County Sheriff's department. A portion of his story is recounted in Chapter Ten, "Day is Done." My own great-uncle, Sheriff Daniel Clayton Adkinson, likewise died while in service, killed April 7, 1938. His wife, Celia Adkinson, succeeded her husband as sheriff for a time, and is a main character throughout this collection of stories. Finally, Sheriff Robert E. Gatlin (1941-1942), was shot and killed by a bootlegger on November 12, 1942.

These men – along with their living
brothers and sisters of the badge – represent
the sacrificial, heroic character that has
transformed "Wild, Wild Walton" into a safe,
welcoming community for tens of thousands of
full-time citizens and hundreds of thousands
of visitors each year. The Walton County
Sheriff's Office aspires to see that their
sacrifice will never be forgotten. And I hope
this little book goes a long way in preserving
and honoring their memory.

Sheriff Michael A. Adkinson, Jr.

AUTHOR'S PREFACE

In the winter of 2015, I accepted the invitation to write the stage play for the annual production of "Grit & Grace." "Grit & Grace" is Walton County's official folklife production, whose mission is to preserve the oral history of the greater community.

Admittedly, I was a novice, for while writing has been a large part of my vocation for more than a decade now, playwriting was a brand new challenge. But with incredibly rich "raw material" and the support of veteran participants in "Grit & Grace," the play came together like a tightly constructed puzzle in one of the most enjoyable writing projects I have ever undertaken. Consequently, when the "Grit & Grace" Board of Directors asked me to produce a book based on the 2015 play, I was more than eager to oblige. The book you hold in your hand is that product.

Since this is an adaptation, a few notes of explanation are in order as you begin reading.

First, this book is not identical to the play that preceded it. These two works should be seen as companion pieces, not duplications, as each piece contains unique materials. There are common characters and common stories to be sure, but each production stands alone.

Second, this text contains a combination of both historical and fictional characters.

ix

The actual, historical characters are presented with the aid of written accounts, personal interviews, and known facts, though creative license is utilized. Fictional characters are presented to aid in the easier flow of the stories.

Third, the chapter endnotes are an integral part of the stories themselves. I have chosen to include them at the end of each chapter – rather than at the end of the book – to make it easier for the reader to gain additional information and context.

Finally, it's worth making a point as to why works like these matter. Simply, there is so much to learn from the past.

We all have heard the bromide that those who fail to remember the past are doomed to repeat it. That statement is true, but it is often mangled beyond usefulness. The actual quote belongs to George Santayana, and his words in their entirety, are even more robust. He said, "Progress depends on <u>retentiveness</u>. When experience <u>is not retained,</u> as among savages, infancy is perpetual. Those who cannot remember the past are condemned to repeat it" (emphasis added).

Thus, "Wild, Wild Walton" is an apropos title. For if we do not revisit and retain the experience of our community's raucous past, indeed, we will collapse into savagery once again, in spite of our contemporary setting and ideals. Or, put plainly as my Appalachian grandmother often warned me: "Don't forget yer raisin' lest you get too big fer yer britches."

Dr. Amy A. Kass, who taught at The University of Chicago before becoming a Senior Fellow at the Hudson Institute, often told a story she heard from her mother's rabbi. A mother bird and her three hatchlings came to the banks of a mighty river, a river too wide for the young ones to fly across on their own. Taking the first one on her wing, the mother bird began to carry him across while the others waited on the other side.

While over the middle of the river she asked him: "My dear son, when I am old and too feeble to fly, will you carry me across the river?" Her son answered, "Of course I will, mama." The mother bird promptly dropped him into the water. Repeating the test on the next little one, she asked, "My dear son, when I am old and too feeble to fly, will you carry me across the river?" He answered, "Of course I will!" He too, was unceremoniously dropped into the river.

Gathering up her last youngling, the mother bird asked the question one last time: "My dear son, when I am old and too feeble to fly, will you carry me across the river?" This last little guy didn't answer immediately. But after some thought he finally said, "No mother, I will not do that for you. But I will do it for my own children." This was the right answer. The mother bird flew her son across the river and placed him on the other side safe and sound.[1]

That is a story about rightly appreciating the past, and how it keeps pushing us toward the future. After all, we should be grateful and mindful of the past; it has brought us all to where we are today, and without it, we would not exist. But the proper appreciation of it is to go forward, and to do for the future what the past has done for us – carry us onward.

That Minnesotan treasure Garrison Keillor, who is now in his mid-70s and going as strong as ever, imparts more inspiration and genius than a library full of books. He has never been better than when he said, "The key to cheerfulness is forward movement. Keep moving. Keep knocking. If the door doesn't open, move on. The future has a place for you, and you will know it when you get there."[2]

Maybe this book, in its own little way,
will help you find your way into the future
- by knocking on a few doors of the past.
Press on.

Ronnie McBrayer
Freeport, Florida
June, 2015

1   Dr. Cass contributed this story to "The Giving Tree
    Symposium," 1995. It is available online at
    www.firstthings.com/article/1995/01/002-the-giving-
    tree-a-symposium.

2   Garrison Keillor, January 13, 2014. The Marina Civic
    Center, Panama City, Florida.

TOWARD THE RISING SUN

She drove into the coming light, the early
morning sun not yet breaking the horizon.
Along a gray road that ran like graphite over
green paper, Celia Adkinson was making her
regular hours-long journey from Pensacola
to Live Oak, her Chevrolet Delray pointed
confidently toward the east.

Her route, following old US Highway 90 the
entire way, crawled in and out of piney woods,

01

traversed slow-flowing, lazy rivers, and slid
beneath the boughs of oak trees centuries in
the making. This road passed through the state
capital of Tallahassee and through every
county seat in the Florida Panhandle. It rolled
through cities and townships named after long
dead timber barons and railroad executives.
Places named Pace... Chipley... Bonifay... Sneads.
And of course, DeFuniak Springs.

For the longest time, DeFuniak was no
town at all. It was a primordial hunting and
fishing ground for the Creek, Muscogee, and
Euchee peoples of the Gulf Coast. With its thick
inland forests, fresh water streams, and short
distance to the Gulf of Mexico, the body of
water called "ue hvtke" by some native tribes,
it was surrounded by a primitive paradise.
The survey team of the Pensacola Railroad
recognized this immediately when they first
stumbled upon the site in the late 1800s. So with
an almost perfectly round mile-wide lake as
the centerpiece, the town of DeFuniak Springs
was quickly organized and the railroad had a
brand new stop in Northwest Florida.

Celia knew DeFuniak Springs exceptionally
well, and though she passed through the town
every few weeks, she had not lived there for
some twenty years, and rarely did she stop
anywhere within its city limits. Even on this
morning, as her big Chevrolet glided by the
Walton County courthouse with its white marble

and four massive classical columns, she turned her head away. She just couldn't bring herself to do otherwise, not since she left this town with her three children all those years ago.

This did not mean that DeFuniak was only a painful place for Celia, far from it. She and her husband, Daniel Adkinson, had enjoyed many happy years in the charming little town by the lake, and all three of their children – Tinson, Annell, and Joyzelle – had been born there. Celia had concentrated on raising the children, and Daniel or "Clayton" as he preferred, had worked in that very courthouse that Celia now avoided. Clayton was beloved, respected, and considered a man of great integrity. So, in 1937 when the sheriff's election was held, it was no great surprise that Clayton ran for the office. Neither was it a surprise, when all the votes were counted, that he had won. As a result, the Adkinsons were poised for many happy years with Walton County, Florida as their home. But it was not to be.

As the DeFuniak Springs city limits sign faded in Celia's rearview mirror, once again she let her mind wander back to that evening when her life came unwound. It had been a beautiful spring afternoon on the DeFuniak lake yard. The azaleas were ablaze with crimson while the dogwoods bloomed soft and pink. The oaks shook playfully in the April wind and

every bird, for a thousand miles it seemed, was
overhead making a return trip to the north.
The family's bed sheets were flapping on the
clothes line, the breeze unfurling them like
bleached flags, as the Adkinson children ran
in and out between the posts. Celia had let
them play like this as she worked her flower
beds waking to the warming spring. She scolded
them only slightly when they reached for the
clean sheets with their little, soiled hands.

At evening Celia prepared a fine supper,
fed the children, and then settled at the now
clean kitchen table to help her two oldest with
their schoolwork. Clayton hadn't arrived home
for the evening meal, but this was nothing to
be alarmed about, as he was often late. There
were always mountains of paperwork at the
office, a number of warrants to sign at the
courthouse, or a late day meeting with a judge
or one of the deputies. It was all part of a
sheriff's duty, and Celia understood this.

It was just about dark when the old phone on
the wall rang; its double bells clanging like
a fire engine. Even now Celia could remember
the startling, foreboding dread that seized
her in that moment. The phone routinely rang
in the evening, but on this night, her husband
not yet home, and somehow she knew something
was wrong; and she knew it was Clayton. It
took every ounce of strength she had to place
Tinson's school pencil on the table and to walk

slowly to the ringing phone. She reached for the receiver, a tiny brass and wood earpiece that suddenly seemed to weigh a hundred pounds.

"He-, he-, hello," she said, her voice a tremble.

"Mrs. Adkinson," the serious voice on the other end of the line said. "I'm sorry, but I have the awe'flest of news for you and the chil'ren."

Before the deputy on the line could finish speaking, Celia had collapsed to the floor in shock. Tinson and Annell leapt from their studies and hurried to their mother. Joyzelle, only seven at the time, kept a careful distance. Her huge baby doll eyes were affixed on the phone receiver, now swinging like a pendulum on a chain against the clapboard wall.' Within minutes there was knocking at the door, squad cars in the driveway, a chorus of anxious voices on the front porch, and the Southern parade of kind but awkward words, somber Baptist preachers, and fresh casseroles that are somehow meant to assuage the pain of the heart by filling the belly.

Sheriff Daniel Clayton Adkinson had been at the home of a prison guard discussing an upcoming case when both men were suddenly ambushed by the County Constable. The Constable, who had recently been arrested for operating and protecting an illegal moonshine still, knew that the Sheriff and the prison guard would be testifying against him at his upcoming trial. Unable to face justice, in fear of losing his job, and wishing desperately to be sheriff himself, the Constable, in a despicable act of cowardice, shot the two officers in the back, killing both men. Sheriff Adkinson was 40 years old and had only served in office for a little more than a year.[2]

Lost in her thoughts for the longest time, Celia was in Marianna before she became aware of how far she now was from DeFuniak, almost unconscious of the miles she had driven. The sun was now gloriously high in the sky and the Florida landscape was a cacophony of brilliant, reflected green not yet diminished by the waning year. Halfway to her destination of Live Oak, she would be there in time for lunch and would share the meal with her young friends. Every few weeks Celia made the five-hour drive across the most northern part of her state to spend time with the boys living at the Florida Sheriffs Boys Ranch, and rarely did she miss a trip.

It had been the summer of 1957 when the Florida Sheriffs Association, with nothing more than $5,000 and 140 acres, got to work on an experimental, innovative effort to help troubled kids. It was the Association's dream to create an agricultural retreat where needy, wayward, or neglected boys could grow into strong, lawful, productive citizens who would make positive contributions to their communities. Celia was right in the middle of this effort, and not simply because her fallen husband had been an elected sheriff. She too had held the office, only the second woman in the entire state of Florida to have had the honor.

On Easter Monday, April 18, 1938, just days after Clayton's funeral, Governor Fred P. Cone appointed Celia Adkinson as the Sheriff of Walton County, Florida, a position she held for more than a year.[3] And it was no ceremonial appointment by Governor Cone, either. Celia was the acting, legitimate sheriff who supervised the department, carried a badge and a service revolver, and fulfilled the duties as well – even better – than many of the men elected to the same office over the years. Now, almost two decades after she and her late husband's time in office, when the Florida Sheriffs Association needed help with this project to keep young boys out of delinquency, former Sheriff Celia Adkinson was happy to once again shine her badge and pick up the mantle of dedicated service.

So it was that every few weeks she pushed that Chevrolet east out of Pensacola onto Highway 90 and toward the Boys Ranch. The trunk of the car was always loaded full with home-baked goodies, books for the boys to read, pictures of her own family to share, and of course, her flannelgraph board. She used the fuzzy board to tell Bible stories to the boys, depicting the great tales of Noah and the Flood, Jonah and the Whale, Joseph and his Coat of Many Colors, and Jesus teaching and healing in Galilee. The characters would come alive, their likenesses velcroed to the flannel as Celia told the epic stories, the boys hanging on her every word.[4] To be with these children in the autumn of her life, this is what brought Celia Adkinson back through the city of DeFuniak Springs time and time again.

Remarried, enjoying her grown children and the first of her grandchildren, involved in her church and community, Celia was happier than she had ever thought possible after that dreadful April night in 1938. Consequently, many of her well-intended but nosy neighbors couldn't understand why she went to all the trouble of crossing the state for a few hours of story-telling to children who didn't seem to care. After all, she didn't have to spend hours on the road week after week, riding off into the Florida wilderness for the sake of mostly forgotten boys. She didn't have to continually pass through the beautiful little town that brought back so much personal pain. But really what choice did she have, Celia thought to herself, if she was going to keep loving and keep living?

"You have to take the good with the bad,"

she'd tell the young boys at the ranch her spying neighbors in Pensacola. "And just because you've had some trouble, that don't mean you lay down and die."

So, she just tucked her heartache right there in the trunk with all those home-made goodies, the colorful stories of faith, the smiling faces of those she loved, and the joy of days remembered. Toward the rising sun she carried it all, pressing on, turning her head from her pain when she had to, and lingering in the places where her stories and love could do some good. Somehow, this gave her the resilience to face each new day. Somehow, this filled her with the hope of leaving the world a little bit better than she found it. And somehow, this kept her going back time and time again.

1   The author is indebted to Mrs. Joyzelle Adkinson Gilmore for describing the notification of Sheriff Adkinson's death. Joyzelle is the daughter of Daniel and Celia Adkinson: Joyzelle A. Gilmore, telephone interview with author, April 16, 2015.

2   Ibid.

3   "Widow To Be Appointed Sheriff," *Panama City News Herald*, April 16, 1938, Page 2.

4   Ibid. Gilmore.

WILD WILD WALTON

GRITS

The Florida Sheriffs Association Boys Ranch sat on the banks of the fabled Suwannee River just north of the city of Live Oak.

> "Way down upon de Swanee Ribber;
> Far, far away. Dere's wha my heart is turning ebber.
> Dere's wha de old folks stay."[1]

Stephen Foster wrote those words a hundred years before the ranch was organized, and here, there were no old folks except for the occasional visitors. A few dozen young boys called this spot along the river home, and if all went well, this would not be where any of them would stay. They would learn some agricultural skills, how to work with animals or the land, earn a high school diploma, and launch into the changing world that was the emerging 1960s.

To get to the ranch and its traditional-looking entry marker lined with budding live oaks, Celia turned onto a small two-lane road named after a man as recognizable in these parts as the Suwannee River itself: Mr. Cecil M. Webb.

Cecil Webb was a poor Georgia boy from north of Albany who had moved to Florida right in the teeth of the Great Depression. He had been too destitute to finish any sort of school and had too weak of a heart to continue his promising baseball career. Thus, he started selling dairy products and milled goods door-to-door. It was hard work, but within a decade he had scraped together enough money – saved, borrowed, and otherwise – to form the Dixie Lily Milling Company and was selling grits all over the South.

"Everybody got to have grits," Cecil would say, and it must have been true, as the Webb fortune and fame flourished.

An unwavering man, in addition to his grits empire, Cecil M. Webb owned a semi-pro baseball club, he preached two dozen Sundays a year in Baptist churches across the South, was a staunch land and game conservationist, and he was a legendary host to his friends, locally and nationally.

The story was told, and Celia knew it well, that over time Webb became friends with some of the most powerful people in the country, often sending generous gifts. As a matter of Southern courtesy, he began sending weekly packages of fresh ground grits to President Dwight D. Eisenhower in Washington. Eventually old Cecil had the opportunity to meet the president. It was on St. Patrick's Day 1954, and Webb brought Eisenhower the usual package of grits, a box of cigars, and an uncanny idea: The interstate highway system.

So it was that a couple of years later in the summer of 1956, the Dwight D. Eisenhower System of Interstate and Defense Highways was inaugurated – the greatest public works project in the history of the world. Even as Celia turned off Highway 90 to proceed to the ranch, the concrete of the newly established Interstate 10 was being poured outside of Jacksonville and was moving westward with each passing day. Remarkably, the road was planned to extend all the way to California.

Ike got the credit, but all the old folks on the
Suwannee River knew that the scrappy grits
tycoon Cecil M. Webb had more to do with it
than any Washington politician.[2]

It was also in 1956 that the Boys Ranch began
to take on its current shape. Florida Sheriffs
Ed Blackburn, Ross Boyer, Don McLeod, Hugh
Lewis, and others organized the enterprise,
purchasing or wrestling loose the Suwannee
acreage, and overseeing the construction of
the first buildings. It was a worthy, heroic
idea these men had, to help "straighten kids
out" before they could become serious law
breakers – prevention was always better than
intervention. But being an innovative program
that was severely underfunded, the ranch more
than once faced closure in its earliest years.
Celia would often depart for her drive home
to Pensacola wondering if the doors would
still be open when she returned. No doubt, the
place would not have survived without local
residents doing things like supplying a side
of beef for the boys' meals from time to time,
or anonymous donors paying the ranch power
bill and the like.

Just when the ranch reached its financial
bottom, help arrived thankfully, in the form of
one Harry Weaver. A former teacher, juvenile
services counselor, and federal probation
officer, Weaver had the exact skill set the
ranch needed to pull itself back from the edge

of bankruptcy. With him as the new director, Celia knew the ranch's future was brighter than it had ever been before. She could make that drive with confidence now, knowing that when she came back every few weeks, there would be something to which she would return.

It was Mr. Weaver that Celia first saw, standing in front of the Saunders cottage, as she came down the dirt driveway of the ranch.[3] The driveway, washed repeatedly by tropical rains only to be baked dry by the oppressive Florida sun, was rippled like a washboard, causing the heavy Chevrolet to bounce along as if riding on a railroad bed. Celia managed the undulations and parked, but before the dust could settle, half a dozen little boys were at the doors of her car squealing and laughing with delight. Dirty hands, wet lips and noses, sweaty foreheads and cheeks; all of these were pressed against the car glass. Celia laughed warmly and waved as Mr. Weaver gently ordered the boys away from the car.

"Quit a lickin' the winders or you'll be washin' that car instead of eatin' your lunch," he called out to the boys.

They all immediately retreated several steps away from the car though their eagerness did not dwindle in the least. They loved it when "Ms. Celia" arrived with her goodies and stories, and they loved her. Mr. Weaver knew this as well, so he didn't want to chastise them too severely. While extremely disciplined, Harry Weaver was a patient, soft-spoken man. He had a keen understanding of human nature, as a man of his experience would, and likewise, he knew that these boys had not arrived at the Sheriff's ranch because they were Eagle Scouts. Every one of them had been in trouble, or been troubled in some way, and each boy had a dossier that read like a social worker's nightmare. When they had something to laugh about, to truly enjoy, he could never squash that jubilation.[4]

Of the three dozen or so boys currently at the ranch (the number could fluctuate wildly from month to month), Celia spent the majority of her time with the younger boys, those that were not yet teenagers. It wasn't that she wasn't tough enough to go toe-to-toe with the older boys – she could stand her ground against anyone – she simply enjoyed the impressionable nature of these elementary-aged children. They took to her stories immediately, and there was an openness with a young child that could never be found in a teenager or adult.

"Such is the kingdom of God," Celia thought, and she smiled anew at the boys as she exited her car.

"Ms. Celia! Ms. Celia!" all the little boys were screaming at the top of their lungs. Two boys, Bobby Wills and Raymond Orr, ran straight to open the Chevrolet's trunk, knowing

it was filled with cookies and sweets. A couple
more of the children simply ran straight to
Celia and threw their arms around her waist,
hugs she happily returned.

"Did you bring those sugar cookies like you
promised?" one boy asked.

"Yes, child, you know I did," Celia answered.

"What about the brownies, Ms. Celia? Are
they' brownies this time?" another called while
jumping up and down.

"Yes, yes, just for you, Mikey!" Celia beamed.

The squeals and laughter returned en masse
as the trunk of the car was opened and the
treasure trove of sweets and gifts were carried
to the cottage. As the boys scampered in with
their arms full, Mr. Weaver steered them along
with a firm but quiet voice. Celia took a
moment to look around at the ranch. Again she
smiled.

The place looked better than ever. The
fence rows were meticulously well-groomed. An
autumn garden was vigorously growing. The
foundation of a new cottage was staked out in
the distance. There were several head of cattle
in the pasture, chickens scurried to and fro,
and a pecan orchard would soon be ready to
start dropping its drupes to the ground. The
Boys Ranch was now an actual working farm,
and it made Celia happy.

"It's looking better ever' day," Harry Weaver
offered, watching Celia take in the sights.

"Yes, Mr. Weaver it is. I am so proud – and you should be, too – to come so far in so short of time," Celia answered.

"There's still a long way to go, you know, I tell you. But we'll get there sooner or later." There was optimism in Harry Weaver's voice. There always was.

"Are you ready for a bite to eat? We better feed these young'uns 'fore they founder themselves on cookies and such."

"I am famished, Mr. Weaver," Celia answered. "My breakfast gave out some time ago."

"Well, good. We got some fried chicken fresh from the grounds here. The older boys have been keeping a coop, and as you can see, they've been quite successful. They's yardbirds runnin' ever' where. So we rounded up a few and dressed 'em for lunch."

"That will be lovely."

"Yes ma'am, an' I hope you like grits. Farmer Duffy who lives across the river over there loves these boys the same as you. He don't ever spend much time here at the cottage, but he's always a sendin' somethin' for the table. Back in the summer he dropped off 200 pounds of fresh milled grits and we've been eatin' on 'em most ever' meal since. I hope that suits you alright." Weaver was almost apologetic in his tone.

"Mr. Weaver," Celia answered as she walked toward the cottage door, "that suits me just fine. Everybody got to have some grits, you know."

Mr. Weaver laughed heartily. "Yes ma'am they sho' do, and we got plenty of 'em to go around."

1 Stephen Foster, "Old Folks at Home," 1851. This song, with expurgated lyrics, has been the Florida State Song since 1935.

2 "Dixie Lily Man Was Enamored With Bold Plan," *The Florida Times-Union*, February 13, 2000, accessed online May 1, 2015.

3 The Saunders Cottage at the Florida Boys Ranch is named in memory of Sid M. Saunders, Sheriff of Pinellas County, Florida. The cottage was dedicated in 1958. See photos at Florida Memory, www.floridamemory.com/items/show/75631. See page 134.

4 For a concise reading of Harry Weaver's extraordinary management style and personality, see Simon Slavin and Dennis Young, *Casebook Management for Non-Profit Organizations* (New York: Haworth Press, 1985), 156-170.

LET ME TELL YOU A STORY

When the meal was over, and each child had eaten what seemed like ten pounds each of Celia's cookies, teacakes, and brownies, the boys cleared the table and did the dishes. Taking care of their living quarters and doing their chores was basic to living at the ranch, especially when they had company, even company as familiar as Ms. Celia. With

everything tidied up, Mr. Weaver headed out
to check on the older boys as the youngsters
settled into the living room for story time,
their eyes somewhat heavy from the swelling
grits and sweets in their bellies.

Celia assembled the easel and the flannelgraph
board, placing them in the center of the room.
In her leather satchel was a collection of
letter-sized envelopes, each one with the
cartoon characters of a specific Bible story
inside. One envelope held the Nativity scene
complete with magi, shepherds, and the Christ
child. In another was the prophet Elijah as
he battled the followers of Baal on Mount
Carmel in a fire-lighting contest. The Apostle
Paul's conversion, Jesus feeding the 5,000, the
Creation account – every major biblical story
was in an envelope it seemed, but Celia had
already made her selection. Today, it would be
Daniel in the Lion's Den.

Pulling the caricature of Daniel from his
manilla-colored resting place, Celia attached
him to the light blue flannel board. He was
kneeling, obviously praying, and Celia read:
"Daniel went home and in his upper room, with
his windows open toward Jerusalem, he knelt
down on his knees three times that day, and
prayed and gave thanks before his God."¹

Bobby Wills, one of the boys who had first
helped unload the trunk of the car, spoke up
with his hand raised.

"What was Daniel prayin' about?" he asked.

"Well," Celia answered, as if expecting Bobby's question, "Daniel prayed three times every day – morning, day, and evening – to thank God for all he had, and to show the people watching him that he wasn't ashamed to do the right thing."

"Who was watchin' him?" Bobby demanded.

With this question, Celia reached back into the envelope and then placed a number of ominous looking characters on the blue felt alongside Daniel, peering through the window at him.

"These men here," Celia said, pointing at the villains of the story. "They didn't like Daniel..."

"Why not?" Bobby had to know.

"They were jealous of him, Bobby. You see, the king had made Daniel their boss, but they had a big, wide mean streak in them, and they didn't want him telling them what to do. So they decided to get rid of Daniel for good. They tricked the king into making a law that said nobody whosoever could say their prayers – not even in their own house – so they were watching Daniel to trap him and turn him in."

Now little Raymond spoke: "My granny said they's gonna make it illegal to pray in school someday."

Celia was measured in her response. "That might happen, I suppose, but Daniel's story is somewhat different. If you were caught praying, even where someone said you shouldn't be praying, they would only tell you to stop. But Daniel was thrown into the lion's den!"

Celia moved Daniel's opponents to the upper left corner of the board so they could look down on him in the den. Then, she reached into the envelope again and produced six ferocious lions. She encircled the still praying Daniel with them and continued her story: "They brought Daniel and cast him into the den of lions and left him for the night. The king arose very early the next morning and went in haste to the den of lions. He cried out to Daniel, 'Daniel, servant of the living God, has your God been able to deliver you from the lions?'

"Then Daniel said to the king, 'My God sent His angel and shut the lions' mouths, so that they have not hurt me, because I was found innocent before Him; and also, O king, I have done no wrong before you.' So Daniel was taken up out of the den, and no injury whatever was found on him, because he believed in his God."

The boys wondered at this for a few quiet moments. It was a freckle-faced boy named Charlie who broke the silence.

"So, Daniel was a good guy?" he asked.

"Yes, he was," Celia answered, "he always did the right thing."

"Like Lucas McCain or Wyatt Earp?"

Celia chuckled. "I suppose you could see it like that."

Mikey picked up on the theme. "So them fellers who was out to frame Daniel was like a bunch of Black Barts or the James Gang!"

This realization electrified the room. All the boys erupted with giggles and shouts, pointing loaded fingers with cocked thumbs at one another or throwing shadow lassos as if suddenly transformed into range-riding cowboys.

"Settle yourselves down," Celia had to shout above the fray, and finally she achieved a tenuous calm. But rather than correcting the boys, she followed their thoughts, fiddling through her envelopes until she found the one labeled, "Solomon." From that envelope she produced the horses of Solomon's famed stables and attached them to the flannelgraph board alongside Daniel to the delight of all the boys.

"There," she said, "nothing like a few horses to make things a little more like the Wild West. So yes, Charlie, Daniel was a good guy. He would have worn a white hat had he lived in the American West." Impulsively, the boys cheered. "And Mikey, the men who wanted to get rid of him were like black-hat-wearing outlaws who wished they could run the sheriff off and have their own way with the town after he was gone." At these words the boys booed and hissed Daniel's opponents.

Bobby returned to his questions: "Ms. Celia, were you around durin' the days of the Wild West?" and Celia couldn't help but let out a hoot at such a question.

"Lord, son, just how old do you think I am?" Celia answered as she and the boys laughed together. "No, no, no, I might be old enough to be your granny, but I'm not near old enough to recall those days."

Undeterred, Bobby continued: "Well, do you know any stories from the Wild West? I mean, these Bible stories are good and all, but they ain't got no John Wayne in 'em or nothin'. Could you tell us some of those stories?"

"To tell you the truth, Bobby," Celia replied, "You probably know all the same stories I do. All of you have read about 'Hopalong Cassidy,' haven't you?"

"Yes ma'am, we have!" came the answer.

"And you've seen the 'Red Ryder' and Roy Rogers comic strips, right?"

"I got a whole shoe box full of them!" one of the boys hollered out.

"And I know you've watched more 'Gunsmoke' and 'Lone Ranger' than I have?"

With this shooting, romping, horseback riding, and lassoing overtook the room once again, and Celia realized she had better tell some kind of Western story or the afternoon would be lost, with or without the flannelgraph board.

So after settling the boys down one more time, Celia dragged a large easy chair to the center of the room, and abandoned her usual posture of standing while she told the Bible stories. No sooner had she sat down than all the boys began to gather at her feet like chicks around a mother hen, their eyes aglow with anticipation.

"For many years," she began after taking a deep breath, "I lived in a place not far from here called DeFuniak Springs."

"Dee-funny-what?" Raymond asked, unable to stop himself.

"DeFuniak," Celia repeated quietly. "It is a sweet little place named after a man who worked for the railroad. It is filled with long rows of cute houses, and there is a giant, perfectly round lake right in the middle of town with fish in it, Ray, longer than your leg. And there on the main street is a new courthouse bigger and prettier than any building you have ever seen. That courthouse is there," and now Celia lowered her voice to just above a whisper and leaned forward in her chair, "because some scoundrel burned the first courthouse down, and nobody ever found out who did it!"

The boys "oohed" and "aahed" over this information but they allowed Celia to continue.

"You see, DeFuniak is part of a place called

Walton County, and for many, many years the
woods and bayous of Walton County were filled
and running over with cowboys, moonshiners,
thieves, pirates, murderers, and all kind of
outlaws that make some of the folks from the
Wild West - or even the Old Testament - look
like Sunday schoolers by comparison."

"Did you know any of these bad folk?" one
of the boys asked.

"Yes, yes, child I did. I knew a few of the
worst," Celia answered.

"Will you tell us about them?" Bobby asked.
"About the worst?"

"I, I don't know about that," Celia hesitated.
"Some of these stories might give you nightmares
and Mr. Weaver would be mighty upset with me
if all of you were crying to sleep in his bunk
room tonight." With one voice the boys vowed
that they were old and tough enough to hear
about the wild, wild Walton County that Celia
had just introduced. They begged her to tell
her stories until she thought a couple of them
might cry with disappointment if she didn't.

Raising her hands to quieten the boys, she
became more serious, realizing that she was
about to tell tales from a chapter in her life
that she had kept from these precious ones.
But in their faces she saw Clayton, somehow,
and she felt that he would want some things
told lest the stories be lost to the past rather
than survive as living history. Besides, Celia

thought to herself, if children can't be trusted with one's heritage – the good, bad, and ugly of it all – then who is it for?

"Okay, here is the deal I will make with you," she said, and a collective snicker rose among the boys because they knew they had prevailed. "Everything I tell you for the next little while is just between us, because we are friends," she said. "And I'm going to do more than just tell you about the outlaws from Walton County. I'm going to tell you about some of the heroes and good guys too.

"My grandfather would often tell me that everybody has two wolves that live inside of them. One is dark and evil. The other one is good and right. These two wolves are always fighting among themselves, one trying to beat the other. Do you know which wolf will win?" Celia asked the boys who were now listening as if sitting on the mourner's bench at a revival meeting. "The one that you feed," she answered.[2]

"These people I'm going to tell you about were all just like you and me. Just like Daniel and the men who were after him. They all could do the wrong thing, or they all could do the right thing. They had to decide for themselves every day. I want you to hear about them so that you will remember this lesson: Whichever part of that soul of yours that you feed, way down inside of you, that will be the part that wins – good or bad.

"Well," Celia said almost blushing, "that's enough preaching. Boys, let me tell you a story..."

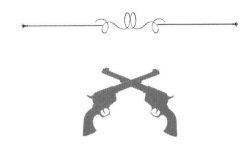

1   For the biblical account, see Daniel 6:1-28.

2   The "Tale of Two Wolves" is thought to be an ancient story from the Cherokee Nation. I first heard it from my paternal grandfather as a child.

THE DEVIL IN A BLUE DRESS

It was early October. Samuel and Joseph
Walden, with stern faces astride lathered
horses, cut a formidable trail through the sea
of blooming cotton. The brothers had ridden
hard all day long, stopping only to water
their mounts and to rendezvous with various

31

members of the former 8th Florida Infantry;
at least those infantry members who were still
living.

The 8th Florida Infantry had been comprised
of young men from the northern part of the
state. Formed almost as immediately as the
shots fired at Fort Sumter, the Confederate
unit was active for the duration of the war
and endured nothing short of hell on earth.
Manassas. Sharpsburg. Antietam. Fredricksburg.
Chancellorsville. Spotsylvania. Cold Harbor.
The Florida 8th was in almost every major Civil
War engagement, including Lee's surrender at
Appomattox.

But for the Walden brothers and the hard-
riding veterans now riding across the Florida
savanna, the war had ended at Gettysburg. They
were all members of Company E and had been
attached to General George Pickett's division
on that fateful July afternoon in 1863. Of
the more than 12,000 confederates who stepped
toward the Union entrenchments that day, more
than half would be killed or wounded in a
decisive defeat from which the South never
recovered. Samuel and Joseph had survived
Pickett's Charge, but were among some 3,000
prisoners of war taken by the Yankees.

Shell-shocked and exhausted, the brothers
were transferred to the Fort Delaware Union
Prison. The conditions were abysmal. The
Waldens, no longer in fear of life and limb

Florida Civil War Battles AP

on the battlefield, now had to fight off
smallpox, pneumonia, dysentery, and malaria.
Samuel, the older of the two, very nearly
succumbed to death in prison. His health had so
deteriorated after one year, he was released as
part of a prisoner exchange, the Union doctors
concluding that Samuel was probably going to
die anyway. But he didn't. He was taken down
the coast by ship and released in Savannah.
He recovered, then walked the nearly 400 miles
home to Walton County. A few months later,
the war having ended, Joseph returned home as
well.

    The reunion at home, however, was not to be
a sweet one. The summer that Samuel and Joseph
had been charging up the railed Emmitsburg
Road at Gettysburg, their older brother –

Morris – was in his own battle at home on the
Shoal River. Morris was resting at the end
of a long day in the sitting room with his
wife, children, and his parents. The family's
thoughts were on the brothers fighting with
Lee somewhere in Pennsylvania. There was a
noise outside and Morris went to investigate.
A band of "scalawags," or Union sympathizers,
led by a man named Fowler, was waiting on
him. They shot him in cold blood only to steal
his livestock and farming stores. Then they
lingered in the yard, on horseback, waiting
for Morris' aged father to "do something" so
they could shoot him too. Instead, old Moses
Walden ran to his dying son.

And so it was, the Walden brothers
fought their way through one inferno, were
incarcerated in another, and came home to
one further still. When the sparse local law
enforcement could not make a case or arrest the
murderers, and Morris' father-in-law's offered
reward brought no results, it was more than the
Walden brothers could stand. The remnants of
Company E, 8th Florida Infantry reassembled
in their Confederate gray, taking the shape
of a posse, and rode east from Shoal River to
mete out their own brand of frontier justice.[1]

Having experienced days of no success, on
this morning word had come to Samuel that the
scalawag gang was hiding near Lake Jackson
at the Florida-Alabama line. So thundering

across the sandy hills they rode, awash with vengeance, as if charging that Gettysburg hill once again.

As the afternoon sun began its slide toward the horizon, the Waldens arrived just outside a settlement that was quickly becoming known as Florala, situated as it was on the dividing line between the two states. It was a small but busy hamlet that had begun to accommodate men just like the Waldens: Civil War veterans returning home and looking for farm land, forests, and stillness following so much war. This would be a friendly place for the Waldens to investigate the whereabouts of their quarry, but they were wary of showing their faces as they were known by the gang. So two other members of the posse, Levi and Jasper, headed into town while the Waldens and Ben Jones – "Jonesey" they called him – stayed with the horses.

The three men passed the time in silence, watering and brushing their horses, chewing on some jerky and hardtack, and drinking what seemed liked gallons of water from their canteens. They also checked and double-checked their pistols, all three armed with old .44 caliber Colt Dragoons.

"You reckon we got 'em now?" Joseph asked the other men after a while.

"Heck, if I know, but this is the best lead we've had in a spell," Samuel answered, his hand quivering as he tried to steady his pipe for lighting. He had developed a tremor on his left side during that dreadful year in Delaware and it showed no signs of going away.

"Boys, he' 'dey come," Jonesey said, pointing toward Florala. Levi and Jasper were coming at them almost at a run. Their collective pulses quickened and the horses tensed as well, ready for action. Winded, the men arrived and between massive breaths, began to speak.

"We too late fer two of 'em," Jasper offered, trying to slow his breathing. "Two of 'em already dead," he finally spat out.

"Yeah, they got theirs," Levi offered. "A bounty hunter got the drop on 'em over in Geneva and intends on collectin' the reward money from Morris' paw-in-law, Sam."

Samuel slowly nodded his head. He didn't feel the need to personally execute anyone, not even his brother's killers. He was satisfied only that an eye had been taken for an eye.

"Is one of the dead the leader? Is one of them Fowler?" Joseph asked, hoping for the chance to string up his brother's killer himself.

"No," Levi answered, bent over, his hands on his knees.

"That's why we be runnin' sa hard," Jasper squeaked out. "They'd told us wher'd he be livin', and we's got to get on out there to 'im

'fore he packs up an' leaves or any other folk
warn 'im that we's here!"

With this word, all five men mounted their
horses as Levi and Jasper simply started riding
in Fowler's direction, the others following. As
they rode, the details were filled in. Fowler
and his gang had retreated to the piney hills
of Walton County once Morris' brothers had
arrived home from the war, knowing revenge
would be on their minds. There, the three had
begun to farm on Turkey Creek, using Morris'
goods, no doubt, in the process. The two unlucky
members of the gang, whose hides had been
collected by the bounty hunter, had simply
dropped their guard and sashayed into town
as if going to a church picnic. Fowler, much
more vigilant, was keeping a low profile on
his farm. With sinking hearts, the Waldens
knew that Fowler had probably already fled
the country, the news of his partners' demise
being widespread.

In an hour the posse was in the pine
thicket adjoining Fowler's farm, their horses
tied and cobbled some distance away. They
scouted the blooming cotton field as if doing
reconnaissance for Longstreet or Lee. There
was a ratty farmhouse, not much more than
a lean-to, and a barn in equally deplorable
condition. A couple of cows were drinking from
the creek, and when Joseph looked through his
field glasses in that direction, he could see

Morris' brand on their hindquarters. Fowler didn't seem to have any dogs, and outside of the rickety house, there was little place he could hide or defend himself. With the waning sunlight, it had the scent of a perfect ambush, except, there was no sign of the elusive Fowler.

The only person on the property was a woman in a sun bonnet and blue dress, picking cotton just as furiously as she could. The posse settled down in the woods and deliberated over what they should do next.

"I says we go on an' 'terrorgate 'dat ole woman 'dere," Jasper offered. "She'd a know'd where Fowler is."

"No," Samuel replied with a bit of a grimace. "Fowler very well could be in the house, there. If we spook him with our horses a half-mile away, we'll never catch him."

"Sam's right," came Levi's answer. "I say we wait until dark, scurry up on the homestead and take a look inside for ourselves. If's he there, we put him out of his misery. If he ain't, we get what information we can from the woman."

"Well, what you gonna do if he be 'der and you'd a send 'im to 'is Maker and de woman bears wid'ness? What 'den?"

Jasper's question gave the entire group pause. They were keen on killing a murderer but wanted no part whatsoever in shooting or otherwise harming a lady.

As they thought about their next move, Joseph Walden, who had never quit studying the farm with his field glasses, broke the silence: "Almighty, boys! The woman a peacockin' in that cotton field ain't no woman! It's Fowler!"

The men of the posse peered through the coming dusk at the woman in the blue dress. In unison they turned and looked at Joseph, their eyes bugging and their mouths agape.

"Give me that!" Samuel barked, and snatched the glasses from his brother's hand. He looked through the glass, his left hand steady for the first time in a year, and after a moment whispered, "Well, fry my hide."

Without a word or command, Samuel Walden cast aside the field glasses, rose from his spot in the pine thicket, and began walking steadily through the cotton toward Fowler. After the shock of the moment passed, the rest of the posse joined him, forming a line, their shadows from the setting sun stretching toward the bonnet-wearing, blue-dressed cotton picker.

Bent to the ground, frantically picking cotton and stuffing into a sack three times as long as he was, Fowler never heard the posse come upon him. It was Samuel's voice that tore him from his labor.

"Excuse me, ma'am," Samuel said in a soft, syrupy voice. "We were wondering if you knew the whereabouts of the cowardly, murderous, ragbag known as Judson Fowler. We would be obliged for your help, being that we are here to see that he pay for his sins."

Fowler slowly stood, raised his hands from the cotton sack, and carefully turned to face the Waldens and their posse.

"Evenin' gentlemen," Fowler said with a shaky voice while wiping the sweat from his forehead and beard.

"Evening," said Samuel. "You wearing dresses, now, Fowler?"

"Oh, it's easy to explain, Sam," Fowler answered sheepishly. "My crop was in, and I couldn't let it go to seed, you know. And while I figured you boys would be this way soon enough, I needed the money the crop would bring to get on out of here."

"Sort of hiding in plain sight, then," Joseph offered.

"Just like that, Joey, yes sir," came the reply, "'cause I wanted to get my reaping done before the winter."

The men stood, looking at one another, frozen. Only the sound of the mooing cows by the creek breaking the silence. Samuel reached for his pipe. Laboriously, he packed it, the tremor having returned to his left hand. He struck a match on his belt buckle and took a long draw, the sweet smell of cherry tobacco filling the air. At last, he spoke.

"That's the thing about farming, Fowler," he said, taking another long puff from the pipe.

"'Whatsoever a man soweth, that shall he also reap."[2]

The next morning, travelers on the Florala Road reported hearing the sounds of frantic gunfire the night before, though no evidence of any such activity could be discovered.[3]

1   Janet Walden Miller's research project, "Pioneer Corner: The 'Waldens of Walton County,'" provides this factual information, though the name "Fowler" is a dramatic license. See Chick Huettel, Joe Stanko, and Chuck Ebbecke, *History of Walton County Posse* (Santa Rosa Beach, FL: Published by Authors, 2012), 12.

2   Galatians 6:7, KJV.

3   Ibid., *Posse*. The gang leader was aware that he was a target, but put on a dress and bonnet to plow his field, thinking to avoid detection. Once discovered, each member of the posse fired upon him so that no individual could be accused of murder.

SNAKES IN THE SNEAK BOX

Nathaniel carefully pulled a few greenbacks from the hidden pocket of his trousers, making certain that he was not in sight of his "contractor's" prying eyes. He was a seasoned, well-traveled explorer, Nathaniel H. Bishop, but never had he encountered so much treachery as in his last hundred or so miles

43

along the Gulf Coast. He had been waylaid by
pirates, chased through the dark of night by
men intent on killing him and taking his boat,
and he had been forced to contend with some
of the most desolate, forsaken coastline in the
Western Hemisphere.

A good deal of his trouble was simply part
and parcel for the life of an adventurer and
he accepted it well. A child of New England,
he had seen more of the world in his forty or
so years than most men would see in multiple
lifetimes. He had hiked the Andes Mountains
before his high school graduation, and had
paddled thousands of miles of Canadian and
US waterways, including a months-long voyage
down the entire length of the Mississippi
River. Now, here he was halfway along on
another great venture from New Orleans to Cape
San Blas. He was standing with his traveling
companion, Saddles, on the marshy bank of a
body of water the local tribes called "The
Choctawhatchee," preparing his sneakbox[1] and
canoe for portage to St. Andrew's Bay.[2]

"I tell you, Saddles, we must be quite wary of
this man who now maintains our vessels as his
reputation for savagery and his propensity for
larceny are legendary among his neighbors,"
Bishop began. "He is a dangerous man if
anything at all, who by exaction, brutality,
and even worse means, has gotten hold of most
of the cattle, and everything else of value, in

this entire area. One settler near Santa Rosa Island even dared whisper to me that this man is responsible for the assassination of his wife and nephew to claim their inheritance. I mean, who kills his wife for the purpose of gaining a few cows?"

Saddles, whose demeanor was one of natural suspicion, was scandalized. "Well, sir, why have you entrusted our goods to him?"

"Because I had no other real choice!" Bishop thundered back. "We have no carts, no horses. It is several days' sail back to the East Pass, time that I cannot waste; and you saw the desolation of the region as we traveled along. And where there are a few settlers, beguiled here by the sentimental idea of pioneer life in a fine climate – 'The Florida Fever' it's called – these people have fewer rations than we carry in the sneak box. They have a fever, that is certain and sure: Fever that is the product of starvation on a fish diet and blood loss from insect attacks. None of these lonely pilgrims will be able to assist us. Furthermore, this W.D. Holly possesses the only yoke of oxen capable of making the portage to St. Andrew's Bay. I am afraid we are in point of fact, stuck with him for the next fourteen miles."

Both men were silent a moment and Bishop tightened his hand around the dollar bills he had removed from his trousers. Holly and a couple of his hired hands were now approaching, having lashed the boats to an ox-drawn wagon. Saddles leaned over and whispered in Nathaniel Bishop's ear, "I will concede the argument. However, please understand that I will not resist for a moment, if it be required, sending this snake in the grass off to Hades where he belongs." Saddles gave the pistol on his hip a small pat and turned his suspicious gaze to W.D. Holly and his men.

W.D. Holly was a clean, handsome, well-dressed man; tall and striking. Holstered on his right hip was a massive Colt Peacemaker and a Bowie knife just in front of it. On his left side was nothing, as his left arm hung there stiffly, apparently made useless for some unknown reason. Towering in the Florida brush and flanked as he was by his accompanying hired men, he made a most sinister impression.

His voice was low and full of gravel. "You gents about ready to roll along?" he asked.

"Yes, yes, of course," Bishop answered with more nervousness and fidgeting than he would have liked. "Now, Mr. Holly, to the issue of payment as of yet undefined. The portage, in my associate and I's estimation, is worth some $3 or $4 dollars. Yet, in the interest of goodwill and seeing that you have controlling interest of this mode of transportation, I will gladly pay you $5 for your troubles. How does that sound?"

Holly's countenance was unchanged. He only

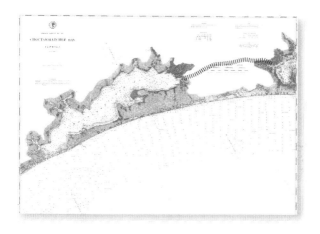

spoke: "Sounds mighty cheap. It'll be $10."

Bishop was startled at the price and Saddles gave a snort. Holly and his men remained emotionless.

"Certainly, I have left room for negotiation with my initial offer. What about $7? How does that strike you, sir?" Bishop asked, beaming a smile. Holly simply spat at the ground, missing Bishop's boot by an inch. His face remained a stone wall.

"Splendid, then! We have an agreement. $10 it is," Bishop answered breaking the tension. With that, the dollars were exchanged and the hired men headed for the wagon with a begrudging Saddles right behind them to keep a watch over their belongings. With whips and ear-splitting cursing, the oxen were put into motion. As Bishop started down the wilderness road, Holly snagged him by the sleeve and spoke in a tone as close to kindness as the man possessed: "How 'bout we have us a bite to eat 'fore plungin' into the palmettos? Wes'll travel much faster than the ox and wagon. Ain't no need to hurry."

Cautiously, and with more than a little trepidation, Nathaniel Bishop followed Holly to a small shack alongside the Bay. It was more of a covered fire pit for cooking than anything else, with a couple of chairs and a table to eat a meal. Holly stepped inside and returned with a large plate of food held by his good arm.

"I tell you, I'm sa' hungry I could eat a scabby mule. Ain't had my breakfast," he said. And taking food from the plate, Holly offered it to Bishop who upon the first scent of it, was repulsed.

"My God, man! What is that wretched piece of meat?" Bishop asked.

"It's gopher, and a mighty good 'un too," Holly answered as he sloppily devoured the animal. "The gopher always comes outta his hole in the early morning to get the dew. You can snare 'im then. Tenderize him in a pot and he'll make a thick brown gravy. Throw in some rice and your tongue'll lick yer lips sa' fast it'll nearly beat ya brains out. 'Course, if you can keep from eatin' 'em all up, you can ship a mess of 'em down to Pensacola for a $1 a body where they eat 'em in the cafes."

Bishop was not impressed. "A $1 a piece?" he asked. "Sir, it is a rodent!"

"Ain't no matter." was the return. "It's good eatin' and good money."

"Well, I am happy to dine with you, but have you no jerky or salted beef?" Bishop asked. "I hear you are somewhat of a cattle baron in these parts."

Holly stopped chewing mid-chomp, fixing a steely gaze on Bishop. He reached for a mason jar with some kind of rank liquid in it, took a long draw and asked, "What, exactly, have you heard about me?"

Bishop, aware that he had crossed into dangerous territory began to backpedal. "Uh, oh my," he nervously laughed, "only that cattle is your business sir, and you are very good at business."

Holly slowly wiped away the gopher gravy that was hanging from his chin with the back his hand. He relaxed, eased back in his chair, and said, "In that regard you'd heard right. I ain't from here. Nobody is. Come here from Mississippi. Back in Mississippi I was a doctor. But what with all the widows and the orphans made by the War of Northern Aggression, they weren't nobody who could pay a bill. So I come here to make my fortune in the river bottoms of Walton County, Florida."

"I see. And if it is not too forward to ask, did you receive your...wound...in the, what did

you call it, 'War of Northern Aggression?'"
Bishop gently asked while motioning to Holly's
damaged arm.

"No," Holly spat quite savagely, as if the
memory of some long ago injury produced pain
in his shoulder all over again. "This here be
the product of one Charlie Bridekirk, a no-
good mischief-maker. He used to live in these
parts."

"Used to, sir?"

"Yep. He's dead. Kilt about a month back.
And I ain't cryin' 'bout it neither. I went
over to his place some years ago to give 'im
a talkin' about some of his doin's. He tried to
kill me - just started blasting away with his
scatter gun - and most of the shot's still in
my shoulder."

"Did you report this man's action to the
authorities?"

Holly gave a snarling laugh, almost
contemptuous. "Authorities? You mean the law?
They ain't much law around here, mister. And
when they is, it's sho' to fizzle out 'fore
gettin' the job done properly. No sir, it's of'en
necessary to try somethin' surer than the law."

"Surer than the law? What is more sure than
the law?" Bishop asked

"Lynchin'," came the answer. Holly stood
as he spoke, smug and bold. "When I come to
these parts I married a widow-woman who owned
most'a this land and a thousand head of cattle

on it. She owned 'em with her nephew, that is.
And that Bridekirk, who'd been squatting on
my lan-, er, uh, my nephew's land, shot the
boy dead one mornin' as he took his breakfast.
We know'd it was him, but we couldn't get no
indictment or sheriff to take up the cause.
Then the grief of it all put his poor aunt,
my wife, in the ground her ownself within a
month. Being a doctor, I am certain that was
the case and would testify to that conclusion.
I was left to hold my loved ones' claim as
their sole heir. And that's how I's got shot. I
went just to talk to Charlie - to make peace
and let bygones be bygones - and he commenced
to shootin'."

Holly paused to rub his wounded shoulder
and arm, then returned to his seat.

Bishop asked, again carefully, "And how long
ago was this incident?"

"Gettin' shot? Been some years."

"Then, after all that time, the alleged
perpetrator of murder and maiming comes to
a lamentable end? Who could have done that?"
Bishop was treading out on thin ice, but
couldn't stop himself.

"I was told that one mornin' last month,
'fore daybreak, Bridekirk and his hired man
heard a noise as though some animal was
worryin' the hens," Holly began. "Old Charlie
stuck his head out of the door, and not seein'
nothin' or nobody, crept on out. Since all the

51

killin' started he'd been cautious somethin'
fierce. Well," and Holly chuckled lightly,
sinisterly, "he weren't cautious enough. They
was two men hidin' behind a hedgerow with
their guns pointed at the door. As soon as
that cow thievin', land-squattin' double dealer
got fairly clear of the door, we… er, – them
fellers, I mean – shot 'im graveyard dead. The
neighbors held a sort of inquest on the case,
but all that is known of the matter is that
he came to his death by shots from 'unknown
parties.'"

As Nathaniel was about to proffer another
question, one of Holly's hired men came riding
hurriedly back down the wilderness road. He
brought his horse to a stop just feet from the
cooking shack and spoke from the saddle.

"Mr. Holly, you're needed down the trail.
The wagon done fell into a big ole suck hole
and the oxen can't pull 'er out alone. We need
everybody what can push'r pull, sir."

Holly stood and gently brushed off his
overcoat and trousers as he spoke to Nathaniel.

"Come along then Mr. Bishop, we got a hard
road to travel." As Nathaniel stood Holly
reached out with his right arm and placed
it firmly on the other man's shoulder. Bishop
turned and looked into the cold, dark eyes
fixed upon him.

"Mr. Bishop," Holly began in that low
gravelly voice, "when there's trouble out here

on the frontier, we have to sort of take care of things on our own. You understand what I'm sayin'?

Nathaniel Bishop, eager to get down the road and be shed of W.D. Holly and his men once and for all answered seriously and quietly: "Yes, Mr. Holly, I do. I certainly do."

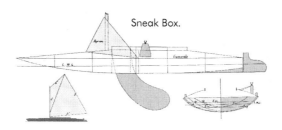

Sneak Box.

---

1 A "sneak box" is small boat that can be either sailed or rowed depending upon conditions.

2 Nathaniel H. Bishop, *Four Months in a Sneak-Box: A Boat Voyage of 2600 Miles Down the Ohio and Mississippi Rivers, and Along the Gulf of Mexico* (Boston: Lee and Shepard, 1879).

FOR FIFTY CENTS

Pauline had the massive patchwork quilt
extended over her lap, falling onto the floor.
It was constructed of pieces of flour sacks,
swatches of calico and gingham, spots of denim
and the occasional string of lace. This was her
latest sewing project, making this quilt for
her youngest daughter who had recently run

55

off and married a boy from Montgomery. The girl's father, Claude, whose snoring from the bedroom sounded as if he were cutting timber for one of the bayou sawmills, was none too happy about this elopement. He thought it rude that he not be asked for his daughter's hand.

"Shoot fire and save the matches, what you 'spect from a boy from Alabama!" Claude had finally reconciled.

For her part, Pauline was tickled. Her daughter had found love, so staying up late to hand prepare this quilted wedding gift, belated as it would be, was no bother whatsoever. And beyond love, there was the practicality of it all. The girl was seventeen and with a husband could make a better living in Alabama's state capital than here in the town of Freeport. Claude worked long days at the landing, loading and unloading all manner of seafaring vessels, and Pauline kept their small farm operating. It was hand to mouth and lots of credit at Ezery Moore's General Store across the street. Had she stayed, as much as Pauline loved her, her daughter's life would not have been an easy one here on Lagrange Bayou.

Pauline stood, carefully stuck her needle in the pin cushion, stretched her stiff back, and gently folded the unfinished quilt to put it away for the night. She was just about to change into her night gown and cap when she heard an awful noise beyond the street. There was banging, crashing, and muted shouts. She stole a quick look at the old grandfather clock in the corner. It was a quarter to one. In the moment it took to tell the time, the disturbance outside only grew louder and more clamorous. Frightened, Pauline turned to call for Claude in the bedroom, but when she turned, there he stood, the noise so fierce it had awakened him – not an easy task after those long hours at the docks.

The couple peered out the window with the greatest of curiosity, looking in the direction of Moore's General Store, the direction from which the commotion had originated. What had once sounded like a hog set loose in a Sunday School was now suddenly and eerily quiet. As they studied the scene, the shape of a man, a man who seemed as large as a blue whale, began squeezing his way out of the store's side window! He had considerable trouble, his size being what it was, but finally he collapsed onto the ground with a thud. Immediately, he gained his feet, and with a speed that beguiled his frame, ran quickly east into the woods.

The racket had awakened the entire street. Men, women, children, and couples began to cautiously gather outside the General Store in various night clothes, most carrying lanterns. It was Judith Blount, that old spitfire not afraid of anything, who finally ventured into the store itself, when she saw that the front lock had been ripped away. Shortly thereafter, she came tearing out the front door, screaming bloody murder, as fast as her ninety-year-old legs would carry her.

"Ezery's dead!" she hollered, so as to be heard all the way to Eucheeanna, "Ezery's dead! His brains've been beat slap outta his head!"

Pandemonium ensued as the news billowed through the crowd and down the street. Some ran to find a doctor, though it appeared no doctor would be of service to poor Ezery tonight. Others went to see if the parson was in town, staying at the room he kept in the church. Someone bolted immediately to William McLeod's house on Alaqua Creek. He was a regulator, the closest thing to a lawman for some thirty miles. A few took to the woods, on the trail of the alleged assassin. Others, reeling from the shock of the news, entered the store to fetch Ezery's body, and grimly brought it out to the street. There, respectfully, they covered him with a blanket and waited for the doctor, preacher, or regulators - whoever came first - with word on what should happen next.

As the crowd waited and wept, they grew more and more angry, filling the air with frustrated questions: "Who would do such a thing as this? Why hurt little Ezery when he'd give someone whatever it was they wanted anyway? How will his wife and children bear this news?" By the time McLeod arrived, riding bareback on his giant, red mule, the small crowd was feverish for vengeance.

Had the circumstances been somewhat different, William B. McLeod's arrival would have been hailed as the vanguard of some circus or side show. Comically, he was dressed in long, white underwear and English riding boots that rose almost to his knees. He dismounted smartly, brandishing a shot gun, draped in bandoliers, and wearing a fine Scottish military hat, a topping he was never seen without. McLeod was a proud Scot – they all are – a direct descendent of the first Scottish families who had settled in Walton County, Florida some 75 years earlier.'

"Ah-right! Ah-right!" McLeod barked at the crowd. "Ye people got to calm down if there's to be any justice tonight. So, hold a minute an' someone tell me what happened here and who's the poor sacket a kipping 'neath the blanket?"

Everyone answered at once in a mighty chorus of confusion, each person sharing his or her unique vantage point of the terrible affair. Finally, McLeod fired a shotgun blast into the air to silence what was quickly becoming a vigilante mob, and began his questioning again. This time, he got slower, more deliberate answers, with Claude and Pauline providing the main storyline, as their house was directly across from the store, while others filled in various details.

"I saw that fat feller a crawlin' out the winder," one said.

"He was the one what came in at the landin' earlier t'day, I believe," another offered.

"That'd be right," still one more witness volunteered. "And he had a partner – a little wormy feller named 'Mink' or 'Meck' – no, it was Monk – Monk, that's it."

"Yessiree, you right," Claude said. "They made anchor at the landin' 'cause I remember how that fat boy 'bout sank the cockleshell they was sailin' just by a sittin' in it."

Pauline joined in with why Ezery was in the store at this time of the early morning, telling McLeod, "Ezery slept in a little room in the back, you know, to keep his sundries safe from thievery just like what's happened tonight. But this is a lot more than thievery, Mr. McLeod. You say you gonna run for sheriff one day, well now's your chance to act like one. That animal killed this boy with his bare hands – and he's gotta pay for what he's done!"

With that, the little mob broke into renewed wailing and demands for justice. McLeod was chambering another round of .10 gauge shot into his Remington when even louder whooping and hollering was heard in the distance. The crowd fell silent and everyone turned in the direction of the calls, all squinting into the darkness. In a moment a single rider arrived.

It was Tavis, a young man that served as one of McLeod's regulators.

"Mr. McLeod, Mr. McLeod!" he yelled as he rode into the center of the gathering. "We got him! We got that no count bushwhacker that beat Ezery's brains out. The boys caught him tryin' to cross Alaqua Creek up in the sand hills!"

The crowd was ecstatic and McLeod called out above the celebration, "Aye, bless ye, lad! Is it the braw-n-big one?"

"No, sir. He's a sawed-off little half-pint that calls himself 'Monkey' or something." Travis laughed at his own joke. "Heck, he ain't much bigger than a monkey! And he better hope he can climb like one, 'cause he'll be swingin' from a tree here directly."

"Are the boys a harming him?" McLeod asked.

"Maybe a little I guess. But he's in better shape than Ezery, I can tell you that!" came Tavis' defiant answer.

In the fury of the questioning and the crowd's bloodlust, Franklin Parish stepped forward to speak to McLeod. Parish was a reasonable man, respected, and principled. Placing a hand on McLeod's shoulder and drawing him close, Franklin spoke quietly: "William, I appreciate what you and your regulators have done tonight, catching this man so quickly and all. But don't you think we should call the sheriff before rushing to judgment?"

61

"Mighty me, Franky!" came McLeod's lightning response. "Sheriff Campbell's over in the valley. It'll take him two days to get here and this be nothing we can't legate on our own, the law being scarce. Pertaining to his guilt, don't fret yer' self; I thank the good Lord we have these taken witness to the whole scene. I assure you, justice will be fair, my friend, but it be swift."

Some in the crowd, catching word of the conversation between Parish and McLeod forcefully agreed with the Scotsman.

"William, please, this is a bad precedent," Franklin began, louder now, defending his position. "If every posse judges and executes its fugitives, then the posses are going to have to have posses! It will be sheer lawlessness!"

"Franklin, yer talkin' mince! It's lawlessness ah' right now - open yer eyes and see! And ah' right now, it ends."

As McLeod finished his pointed answer, a small group of his regulators arrived with the villainous Monk in their custody. Bound arms and feet, he was dusty and bloody, obviously having been dragged by horses for a part of his return trip to Freeport. The crowd erupted once again with demands for the man's head, and Franklin thought for a moment that they would tear the diminutive man limb from limb. But just as they were about to reach a point of no return, McLeod gestured with his shotgun, and the crowd retreated into a tentative silence. Monk was brought forward, still bound, and placed on his knees at McLeod's feet.

"Ah, ye'd be the accomplice to all this malky, aye?" McLeod asked. "Ye'd be the bludger they call Monk?"

Monk was exactly as he had been described. Small, sniveling, and indeed he looked wormy, as if no food he had ever eaten had done him any good. A coif of dark hair sat atop his narrow head and there were scraggly whiskers on the end of his chin. If he was a day over thirty, it would be a wonder, and he bled from bludgeoned lips and gums as he spoke.

"You'd be right to call me Monk, yes sir, but I never murdered nobody - no sir! That was the stupid oaf who shared my boat!"

"So ye admit yer part in this foolery?" McLeod countered, and the crowd burst into a morbid cheer. Monk began to weep. "Oh fer Christ's sake!" McLeod continued. "If ye're hard enough to beat a man to death, be hard enough to tell the tale, won't ya."

Monk, regaining some composure, said, "We only wanted - we needed - the money. No one was supposed to know! No one was supposed to get hurt! No one was supposed to even be there! We didn't know the boy had sleeping quarters in the store!"

McLeod was unfazed. "Well then, how much poppy did you make off yer lucky dip - come on, let's have it."

One of the regulators stepped forward at McLeod's demand and handed the old Scot a couple of coins that had been taken off of Monk, saying, "That was the take from Ezery's purse, sir. It was in this man's vest pocket."

McLeod looked at the two coins in the palm of his calloused hand for what seemed to be the longest time. Each moment that passed he seemed to grow increasingly disgusted, angrier with every second. Finally, in fury, he exploded: "Ye kilt a man fer 10 shillings - fer 50 cents!!! 50 cents!?!? Crivvens Almighty, have ye no decency, man! Yer soul is as black as the Earl of Hell's Waistcoat! An' hell'll have ye when mi finish with yer body!"[2]

The seething crowd now pressed in from all sides, like dogs at the end of some powerful leash, pulling and fighting to be released. McLeod locked eyes for the briefest moment with Franklin Parish who wilted. Franklin knew there was nothing else he could do, standing alone.

To all of this Monk cried for clemency: "But I didn't do it! Mercy, mercy, I beg you! It was Streeter! That's the name of the fool who committed the crime! Thomas Streeter! He's from Geneva. I'm certain that's where you'll find him come the morning - gone up the river to Geneva. I can take you right to his mama's house where he'll be holed up, I swear I can!

Show charity, good sir, please!"

The crowd fell completely silent, as they, the regulators, and Monk converged their attention on the old man wearing long underwear, a Scottish top hat, and standing in the middle of a dusty road in the middle of the night. He contemplated it all for nearly a full silent minute, only the tree frogs croaking along the water. At last he spoke.

"Aye, mi thank ye for takin' witness to what ye saw – an' what ye did. An' as ye've a given the whereabouts of your partaker, ye'll be granted the swiftest of mercy. As they say back in Scotland, 'A clean shirt'll do ye.'"

No one understood what the man meant in the least. To a person, they all looked at him with the most puzzled gaze. It was Monk, ultimately, who was the spokesman for the entire lot. He said, while reaching to dry his blood and tears with bound hands, "I'm sorry sir, I'm not familiar with that expression."

Without hesitation, McLeod leaned over nose to nose with Monk and growled, "It means in a wee bit, yer neck'll be stretched from a tree!"

Monk fainted immediately away and one of the regulators threw a well-fashioned noose around his neck. The crowd eagerly fell in to assist with the grisly work, and Franklin Parish walked home in the dark, unable to bear the scene. For his part, McLeod walked some distance from the hanging tree and reached into his bandolier to produce a small, tin flask from which he took a hard, quick sip. He was joined by Tavis.

"Tavis," McLeod said as steady as ever, "make ready the horses fer the ride to Geneva. And be sure ev'ry lad has plenty of ammunition for the journey. We leave as soon as this dark faff be complete."

"Consider it done, Mr. McLeod," Tavis answered. "Shall I send words of our venture to the sheriff?"

"The sheriff of Clan Campbell?" McLeod asked, almost offended. "Nay, mi lad. Justice is blind, they say. So let's keep the good sheriff in the dark."

1   The earliest white settlers came to Walton County in the early 1800s, and were indeed of Scottish descent from the Carolinas.

2   The murder of Ezery Moore by Monk and Street was regarded early on as the "Fifty Cent Murder." For more information see *History of Walton County Posse*, 23-25.

RAILROAD BILL

It was 160 miles via the Louisville and Nashville Railway from Chattahoochee to Pensacola, 160 miles of dense, Florida Panhandle wilderness. It took almost seven hours to traverse the route by train, but it might take a traveler more than seven days to cover that same distance on horseback. Jungly brush and pine forests, palmetto brambles and swarms of mosquitoes, poisonous snakes and alligators, exposure to Yellow Fever and parasites, cyprus swamps and flooded rivers: It was a body-depleting, spirit-breaking journey. Thus, the arrival of the locomotive was a godsend.

The particular line that ran through Northwest Florida was owned by the Pensacola and Atlantic Railroad, its primary officers being William Chipley and Frederick DeFuniak, both of whom had new settlements named after them along the route. These men, along with other stockholders, cashed out quickly, however, and within months sold the new P&A to L&N – the "Old Reliable" – for some $6 million in capital stocks and bonds. It was quite the investment, especially for a frontier like the Florida Panhandle, but the deepwater port at Pensacola loomed large in the calculations, and profits were soon forthcoming.

None of this mattered to engineer Harvey Blankenship and his fireman, Gunny. These two had held the reins of iron horses all over the South for L&N – Kentucky, Tennessee, Missouri, Georgia – they even kept their train rolling during the Civil War, driving for whichever side possessed the rails on a particular day. Now, here they were as deep in the South as

L&N had ever pushed, cutting through the dark Florida Panhandle on an overnight run to Pensacola.

Gunny, whose job it was to keep the boiler stoked, also stepped to the small passenger car from time to time to play the role of conductor. It was no problem, as the passenger car was immediately behind the tender, with the remaining freight cars shotgunned together in the same order they arrived and were loaded at the Chattahoochee Junction. Gunny was used to wearing different hats, and when Harvey had to step away to the privy, Gunny even donned the engineer cap for a short time. Again, this was not a problem for the usually uneventful, slow, dark ride to Pensacola.

Gunny, however, was at his usual post, shoveling coal into the boiler of the Rogers 2-6-0 engine when Harvey called out to him from the cab.

"Gunny, get up here and lend me your eyes! There's something on the track!"

Gunny ambled forward and peered down the rails into the dark. Sure enough, maybe two miles ahead, was an orange glow, and it couldn't yet be the lights of the DeFuniak Springs station. The two men continued to stare at it as the train chugged along. It was Harvey who came to the realization first.

"Good God, it's a fire!" Harvey screamed out, and immediately he reached for the brake. The

screech of metal on metal pierced the empty
woods and silver sparks rained on the rails
like a thunder burst. Gunny kept his gaze on
the fire ahead, not yet steadying himself, as
he knew it would take half a mile to stop the
thousands of pounds behind him. As the old
locomotive groaned and shimmied to a slower
pace, the glow ahead came into sharper focus.
It was a massive bonfire, burning as high as
the train's smokestack, completely blocking the
track.

At last, the train rolled to a stop, its slatted
cow catcher just yards from the burning log
jam. Harvey and Gunny simply looked at each
other, bewildered at the sight. In all their
years on the railroad, never had they seen
such a thing. For the sake of caution, Gunny
was about to advise a back trip when Harvey
yanked open the cab door to jump down and take
a closer look, but both men suddenly froze.
Stepping over the cab threshold and filling
up the entire frame was a towering black man
wielding a sawed-off shotgun.

The menacing figure, a foot taller than the
engineer and fireman, looked down on the men
with a glower. Then, as unexpected as the fire
on the tracks, he gave the toothiest of grins
and spoke.

"Ev'nin', boys," he said with a chuckle. "My
name be Mow'ris. Mow'ris Slater, and I sho'
pree'shate yun's' co-op'ration." With those words

the big man gave a slight bow and tipped his hat to the men now being held at gunpoint.

"You... You're... You're Railroad Bill!" Harvey stuttered out, with a combination of shock and reverence in his voice, and Gunny knew it was true.

Morris Slater, alias "Railroad Bill," was a living legend in the late 1800s. For years he had made a living robbing depots, freight cars, and train passengers. Kindly, he would collect embezzlements from his victims and then disappear into the lower Alabama woods or upper Florida swamps. There he would subsist on his stolen goods, but largely gave most of it away to the poor, black sharecroppers who, unjustly treated, were only one generation removed from slavery. Bill was hailed as the "Black Robin Hood"[1] by some and thought to be impervious to gunfire by others (save getting shot by a silver bullet).[2] So while he was on the wrong side of the law, Railroad Bill was a hero to his community, and was begrudgingly respected by the agents of the L&N Railroad.

Again, the big man chuckled, this time slapping his thigh with his left hand, before speaking.

"Dat's right, yuns can call me Railroad Bill. Ain't the name my maw gib me, but it suit me fine." Bill turned serious for a moment. "How's 'bout we all mosey on back to dat travel car? I juss need a few thangs fo' I go movin' on, an'

I don't won't no kind of meanness from no'body. Let me do my bid'ness an' I won't hab no need to turn the rest of my boys loose on none of yuns or set fire to no train."

With a gentle motion of his shotgun over Harvey and Gunny's shoulders, Bill pointed to the woods alongside the train. The men turned and looked. Standing along the tree line were a dozen men, bandanas covering their faces, all with torches in their hands.

Harvey swallowed hard, glanced at Gunny whose eyes were as big as china plates, and said, "Well, right this way, Bill."

When they arrived at the passenger car, those on board went into hysterics. The sudden, grinding stop and the acrid smell of smoke had already alarmed them all, especially the majority who had been rudely awakened from sleep. Now, to see a 300-pound bandit come aboard – and a black man at that – had pushed many of these wealthy white travelers right to the edge of sanity. And when Harvey and Gunny explained who the robber was, and pointed to Railroad Bill's threatening gang just beyond the dew-frosted windows, well, any resemblance of dignity was completely lost.

Esteemed business men began weeping like frightened children. More than one woman fainted in a spell of panic. A prosperous cotton farmer soiled his suit pants. A preacher broke into a fervent prayer for God's mercy.

Meanwhile, Gunny opened and emptied the safe, stuffing all its valuables into an old flour sack that Bill had brought along. Then, with the two railmen parading in front of that loaded shotgun, Railroad Bill strolled down the aisle of the train robbing each passenger one by one, always with a "I thank you," or "Pree'shate it," or "'Bliged kine'ly," to those relieved of their goods. Golden necklaces, pocket watches, broaches, and wedding rings: These all went into the bag. If ever a traveler resisted, Bill would simply smile, tip his hat, and motion to his marauders waiting in the woods.

At the back of the passenger car, an old, hard, little woman who was returning to Pensacola, found the nerve to scold Bill for his actions. With the all the bluff and bluster of a schoolmarm, she said to him, "Well, sir, you are a filthy criminal and the devil has certainly taken your soul. That much is sure."

Her words produced a new wave of hysteria within the train and Gunny tried to hush her up himself. Bill, however, sat down beside her, as she had a double seat to herself, his back to the exit, and like a gentleman removed his hat. He motioned for Harvey and Gunny to sit as well, taking open seats near him.

"Ma'am," Bill began, "I ain't been Railroad Bill fo' my who' life. I be a po' mill hand — so po' I'd et my cer'al wid a fork juss to save de milk." Bill gave a bellowing laugh. "But I wucked and wucked till sho' nuff, I'd got holt of the bills fo' a huntin' rifle. But 'dis no count lawman came a lookin' fer me ever' day, showin' up in the cuttin' woods tellin' me I hat to hab a permit. An' dat permit wud caust me more'n ten rifles! An' all dat time they's a hun'derd white men in de woods what didn't hab no permit fer their squirrel guns."

By this time the hysteria of the train had subsided, and the travelers had turned to listen to Railroad Bill's story.

"Well, one thang led to another," he continued, "and dat lawman an' me got to wrasslin' o'ber that confound'it gun at de mill long 'bout supper one night, an' he got shot dead." For the first time since he boarded the train, Bill's jovial smile escaped him. "It wadn't on no purpose, ma'am, but tarnation, won't nobody gonna believe a negro a killin' a deputy! Ain't no way."[3]

Bill stood, his head scraping the top of the passenger car as he returned his hat to its proper place. "You sees," he said with the smile back on his face, "I's kinda got pushed into my line of wuck an' all, but I do confess, I be purdy good at it."

With that, Bill gave the old schoolmarm a wink, and snatched the shiny bracelet off her arm. Turning to the other passengers, he gave a courteous bow, another tip of his hat, and disappeared out the rear door.

The passengers were immediately relieved that Bill was gone, and the preacher who had been once begging for divine mercy commenced an extemporaneous prayer of thanksgiving with several others joining in. The cotton farmer, however, quickly dismissed himself to the lavatory.

Harvey and Gunny, now feeling more responsibility to L&N and less danger from Railroad Bill, carefully exited through the same door that the jovial bandit had just escaped. Of course, there was not a trace of the man, but his ruffians maintained their stoic posture in the woods.

Gunny, his sharp eyes put to work once again, peered out at the men from alongside the train, suddenly feeling as if they were a bit too stoic. He cautiously stepped in their direction with his partner and friend Harvey Blankenship right behind him.

"Get on outta here!" Gunny called, as if attempting to scatter dogs off the front porch. None of the men so much as moved a muscle.

"Hey now, Mr. Harlan's gonna get every one of you!" Harvey added.[4] Still, to a man, no one responded in any way.

With the most measured and guarded steps the two trainmen drew closer to Bill's unflinching, torch-brandishing gang. Again, as on the tracks earlier in the night, it was

Harvey who came to the realization first.

"I'll be dad-blamed," he said aloud.

"Ain't that the darndest thing," Gunny answered.

Smiles that were the combination of admiration, unbelief, and muted frustration crossed the two men's faces. There in the Florida woods, each one sporting a new hat, wearing a bandana, and holding a lantern, were Railroad Bill's nefarious accomplices: Twelve of the most perfect scarecrows Harvey and Gunny had ever seen.

After a few moments Gunny reached out and plucked the closest scarecrow from the ground, took the lantern from its cane pole arm, and started back to the train.

"Where you hauling that thing?" Harvey asked, still taking in the ridiculousness of the entire night.

"To Pensacola," Gunny called back over this shoulder, "cause the bosses at the railroad office will never believe this story."

1   Andy Duncan, *Alabama Curiosities: Quirky Characters, Roadside Oddities and Other Offbeat Stuff,* 2nd Edition (Guilford: GPP, 2009), 2.

2   Kincaid A. Herr, *The Louisville and Nashville Railroad*, 1850-1963, (University Press of Kentucky: Lexington, 2009), 111.

3   See Burgin Mathews, et al (2003, September 3), ("Looking for Railroad Bill"): *On the Trail of an Alabama Badman."* *Southern Cultures*, 66-88.

4   J.B. Harlan was the L&N Railroad Policeman charged with capturing Railroad Bill. While he did not personally apprehend the bandit, he did take possession of Bill's body when he was shot dead in Atmore, Alabama in 1897. Subsequently, Harlan made a spectacle of the man's death, embalming and photographing the body and charging a fee to view the corpse. See Norm Cohen, *Long Steel Rail: The Railroad in American Folksong*, 2nd Edition, (University of Illinois Press: Chicago, 2000), 124-125.

WILD WILD WALTON

CRACKLING COWBOYS

When Celia finished the story of Railroad Bill, her little troupe of listeners was as rowdy as the Freeport mob that had witnessed the arrival of Monk in the custody of the regulators. They were absolutely electrified by the history - their history - but some could scarce believe it to be true.

"Ms. Celia," one of the boys asked, "are you makin' this stuff up just to poke fun at us?" The child was entirely serious with his question.

"Well, son," Celia began, "I know it can be bewildering to look back into time, it all sounding like a crazy Western Show you might see on Saturday morning television. And I said that some of these stories would be hard to take, but every word has been true. Walton County and most of this here Panhandle was as wild as any place the other side of the Mississippi River. Why, if it weren't for men wearing the badge, some standup judges and such, some school teachers to provide some learning and some ministers to give some preaching, it might still be as wild and uncivilized as it once was.

"But considering where we've been," Celia continued, "and considering the shape some of the world is in now, we ought to be thankful that we live in place like this and can call it home. A lot of hard work has made this part of Florida what it is, and a lot of hard work will keep it improving. As you get older, I hope you'll work to make things better - for yourself, and your neighbors."

Quieter now, and remembering a few manners, Charlie raised his hand to ask a question.

"You says the past 'round here was like a Western, Ms. Celia. Was they real cowboys and indians here?"

"There sure were!" Celia answered. "In fact, there are still whole tribes of indians here. American Indians, they prefer to be called – or Native Americans – 'cause they were here first, long before any Spaniards, the French, or Englishmen. There's the Seminole, the Creek, and the Muscogee just to name a few. But I'm sad to say there aren't as many as there used to be. White settlers treated them in the most pitiful fashion: Stole their land, spread disease, and destroyed their way of life..."

"Why would they do some'thun like that?" Charlie demanded.

"Nothing but greed, child, nothing but greed," Celia answered just as quickly, "that's all it amounted to. The Euchee, the Apalachee, large numbers of those tribes that still remain – they were all exterminated, moved out West, or pushed to extinction."

Celia took a serious tone, continuing, "Back in Walton County, just as one example, there was an awful massacre near Alaqua about 150 years ago. Some terrible men got together who were fond of killing the Natives, saying there was a band of Creek braves preparing to attack their settlement. They moved out against the dozen or so 'braves,' but there was only one man among them. The rest were women and children camping along Alaqua Creek and Choctawhatchee Bay. They were all slaughtered and their belongings stolen."[1]

Raymond chimed in, unexpectedly. "My granny says them in'juns all died that way 'cause they were savages and didn't love Jesus."

"Your granny has a whole lot to say, doesn't she?" Celia countered as gently as possible. "It depends upon who is defining 'savage' I suppose. So tell me, little Ray, is it a savage thing to protect your life, land, and property? Or is it savage to kill innocent women and children?" She let that question hang there a moment. "And since you brought up Jesus, I'll ask you another question. What did he say about how we should treat other people?"

With one voice the boys replied, "Do unto others as you would have them do unto you."[2]

"That's right. The way I see it, most of these folks killing and pillaging the Native folks' land sure would not have wanted to have been treated that way. And I'd say a goodly number of them were probably in church every Sunday, but they didn't seem to have been paying the same attention you boys pay." With that, Celia gave a wink to Raymond and continued. "No, most of these folks just wanted to live in peace, like we all do, and why folks couldn't let others be when there was more than enough room and land for everybody, well, I'll never know. But like I said, I hope you'll work to make things better, for yourselves and your neighbors - all your neighbors!"

The boys grew somber and they all were quiet for a while. Their images of the American Indian had been mostly shaped by Hollywood. Thus, the Native tribesman, in their minds, was an uncivilized, war-crazed scoundrel - he was the bad guy. To realize that the "cowboy" was many times the villain, turned their view of things topsy-turvy.

Finally, another hand went up, and another question was asked. This time it was Bobby, the boy who had gotten this whole storytelling session started.

"Surely, there were some good cowboys in Florida?" he asked.

"Oh of course there were, Bobby!" Celia answered. "And here in Florida they had a special name. They were called 'Crackers.'"

The boys all laughed, the unease slipping again from the room, as Celia reached in her bag for a large picture book. She fiddled through the pages as the boys watched and whispered to each other, finally saying, "Aha!" with a smile. She turned the book, as tall as a family Bible, so all the boys could see.

"These are paintings by a man named Frederic Remington," she said by way of explanation, and the boys all pressed in to see. "He was a fine, smart painter who only did pictures of cowboys. You see, he realized that the time of

Frederic Remington, August 1894

the cowboy wouldn't last forever, so he wanted
to capture as much of it as he could, so we
could all remember them. These are pictures of
his 'Cracker Cowboys' from Florida."[3]

"What's a Cracker?" Bobby asked.

"Oh, they are cowboys like no other," Celia
answered with a little mystery in her voice.
"Look at these men in this picture. How are
they different than the cowboys you see on the
television?"

The boys gazed at the picture for a few
minutes, thinking and observing. Then the
answers started exploding like popcorn.

"They ain't got no pistol," one said.

"Their hats ain't Stetsons; they are made outta straw," said another.

"Dogs!" still another hollered. "They got some big dogs wit' 'em."

Mikey almost leapt to his feet as he yelled out, "They all got bullwhips like Lash LaRue!" He was right, and Celia was delighted.

"Exactly!" she said. "Florida cowboys were called 'Crackers' because of the whips they used when driving their cattle. 'Pop! Snap! Crack!'" Celia exclaimed with quick motions of her right hand. "All that cracking must have sounded like fireworks on the Fourth of July. Old Remington, while he painted a few of their pictures, didn't like these 'Crackers' very much."

"Why not?" demanded Bobby, somewhat offended.

"Because they were so unlike the cowboys he knew best from out West."

"How so?" Bobby asked again.

"Well, as you all said, they didn't carry six shooters, only rifles. They kept dogs to help with the herds. They rode much smaller horses and sometimes referred to themselves as 'cow-hunters' instead of cowboys. Remington just couldn't get over these differences."[4]

"Was them Western cowboys better than the Crackers?" It was Raymond's turn to ask a question.

"No, I don't think so. From what I've heard, the Cracker Cowboy horses could stand in bayou

water up to their hindquarters all day and
never have any foot problems - something few
other animals could do. The clouds of mosquitoes
didn't bother them - or their riders - nor
did the heat. Their cows, while not all Texas
longhorns, were part of old Ponce de Leon's
herd, the oldest on this whole continent. And the
Crackers themselves must have been something
to see. Roping bulls at a full gallop while
crossing bayous and snake-infested swamps;
riding through palmetto groves thicker than
bricks; tougher than rawhide on the coldest day;
working their cows in ninety-degree weather,
a hundred-percent humidity, and in the midst
of lightning storms and hurricanes! I'd say
that anyone selling a Cracker Cowboy short
of his Western cousins - even Mr. Remington -
doesn't know the difference between cow patties
and his Crayolas!"[5]

The boys all hooted and howled at Celia's
assessment of Florida's cowpokes and returned
to firing their make-believe pistols into the
air. A couple of the boys added their version
of a Cracker whip, popping and snapping
around the room. Celia let them go at it for a
few minutes and then brought the group back
to some semblance of order.

"Boys," she began glancing at the clock in
the wall, "I'll tell you a few more stories
before we clean up, and then I have to head
back to Pensacola."

The boys gave a collective groan.

"Hush now, if you want me to finish before Mr. Weaver gets back with the older boys," she gently reprimanded. "But these next few stories won't be about what happened all that long ago. I'm going to share a few things I saw with my own eyes. How does that sound?"

The boys cheered with delight and Celia got started once again.

1   John T. Ellisor, *The Second Creek War: Interethnic Conflict and Collusion on a Collapsing Frontier* (University of Nebraska Press: Lincoln, 2010), 382-390.

2   From Luke 6:31.

3   Frederic Remington was a famed cowboy artist and his work included Florida's Cracker Cowboys. The late artist's official website is www.fredericremington.org.

4   See Dana Joseph (2012, December), "Frederic Remington And Florida's Cracker Cowboys." *Cowboys & Indians Magazine*, online at www.cowboysindians.com/Cowboys-Indians/December-2012/Remington-And-Floridas-Cracker-Cowboys.

5   Homeland, Florida has held the "Cracker Storytelling Festival" for nearly three decades honoring the state's folk and cowboy culture. Visit their website at www.crackerstorytellingfestival.com.

BAMBOOZLED ON THE BAYOU

The "Julia Belle" glided gently through
Hogtown Bayou and came avast at the docks
of Cessna Landing.¹ She had steamed in from
Pensacola, as she often did, under the command of
Captain John E. Rogers, making this brief stop
before paddling to her terminus at Freeport.
Indeed, the stop would be only momentary. In
past years, when Cessna Landing was a thriving
port of call with its cafes, saloons, and hotels,

89

the boats were constantly off-loading building supplies, groceries, and people. Now, there were only a few goods to deliver and even fewer travelers.

Yet, surprisingly, today's manifest included a family of four with Cessna Landing as their final destination – the largest number in some time. Captain Rogers looked at the passenger list, as his first mate supervised the mooring of the ship, and then down at the luggage-bearing, trunk-toting family on the deck below.

"The Schellmans," he said quietly to himself. They were elegantly dressed, obviously with some means. There were Andrew and Anna, the parents, with two children: Henry and Kate. Rogers noted that they had listed Pittsburgh as their place of residence, but there was no return trip yet booked. The captain had a fairly good idea why the Schellmans were at Cessna Landing, but like the travelers who had come the years before, it was too late to warn them.

Disembarking with his family and their luggage, Andrew Schellman first noticed that the local town folks were all scurrying about with what appeared to be salvaged boards, recovered planks and tin, and large signs that read, "Cessna General Store," "Cafe," and "Saloon." He hardly had time to think about this state of affairs, however, because the second thing he noticed was the furnace-like

heat – that and the cloud of mosquitos that now
engulfed him and his family.

In the midst of swatting, waving, and
loosening their collars and kerchiefs, it
was Kate who spoke first: "Mother, it is so
desperately warm! Will we be at the resort
soon?"

"I'm sure it won't be long now, darling,"
answered Anna. "Personally, I find these blood-
letting mosquitoes far more of a nuisance than
the heat. But no worries, children, we shall be
away from the elements soon enough. Isn't that
right, Andrew?"

Andrew was now carefully studying a
collection of creased documents he had pulled
from his jacket pocket. He did not respond to
his wife's question.

"Andrew," she repeated with emphasis.
"Andrew, we shall be away from the elements
soon enough. Isn't that right?"

"Oh, yes, yes, my dear," he answered. "I'm
certain Dr. Cessna or one of his assistants will
be along shortly to show us to our quarters.
His instructions on the deed are very clear."
Andrew returned to his documents and read
aloud: "'Upon your arrival at beautiful Cessna
Landing you will be placed in the hospitable
hands of our representatives, escorted into the
lap of luxury, and enjoy world class amenities
at one of our beachside hideaways. Once rested,
and at your leisure, you will be given a tour

of your new estate, replete with orange groves, wild sugar cane, magnificent views of the Gulf of Mexico and Florida wildlife.'"

"That does sound so thrilling!" Anna said, momentarily forgetting the hovering mosquitoes. "Read the part about the farming possibilities!"

"Yes, father, and the hunting and fishing!" said Henry.

"And don't forget the swimming!" Kate added. "Do tell us more!"

"Yes, yes, let's see children. Ah, here is it: 'This land is ideal for fruit growing, orchards, and cattle. There is a luxurious growth of oak, hickory, poplar, sweet gum, and magnolia; and the entire acreage abounds in game. Cessna Landing is perfect for summer homes, game reserves, and with miles of fine water front with high beaches, the bathing and fishing are excellent. Taken as a whole, this is one of the most healthful places in the world.'"[2]

The happy, grinning family looked around at the dilapidated boardwalk, the roughly-dressed passersby with their salvaged goods, and the constant biting mosquitoes.

"This doesn't look like 'one of the most healthful places in the world' to me," Kate said, speaking also for her mother and brother.

"Fret not, child," came Andrew's immediate answer. "I am certain one of the friendly residents of this town will point us in the right direction."

Schellman turned his attention to those passersby hurrying past the docks. Each time he asked for help he was rebuffed, until finally a man carrying a reclaimed plank of wood, plainly dressed in overalls and a large straw hat, stopped to speak to Andrew and his family.

"May I help you?" he asked, lowering one end of the plank to the ground.

"Yes, thank you, my good man. I am Andrew Schellman of Pittsburgh, Pennsylvania – I prospered in dry goods there, you see – and this is my lovely wife, Anna, and our children Henry and Kate."

Immediately the man tipped his hat to the ladies and shook hands with Andrew and Henry.

"It's nice to make your acquaintance," he said. "You can call me Angus."

"Angus?" Andrew asked. "As in the cow?"

"That's exactly right," Angus answered.

"Yes, well, Mr. Angus, being new arrivals in your fair town, would you be so kind as to direct us to the offices of Dr. Charles E. Cessna?"

"Oh, you want to see a doctor? Are you feeling poor?"

"No, no, it's nothing like that, though if these mosquitoes don't let up we may need a blood transfusion!" All the Schellmans laughed heartily at Andrew's joke. Angus, however, did not react.

"Quite right, quite right, yes," he said. "No,

I have purchased a large piece of property from Dr. Cessna and my family is here with me to take possession of it right away."

"Ohhhh," Angus replied.

"Ohhhh?' you say."

"Ohhhh, as in I can't help you," said Angus.

"Well, then, how about his development partner, his brother, Mr. William Cessna? Can you show us to his home or place of business?" Andrew asked.

"Nope."

"'Nope,' you say."

"Nope."

Andrew, showing confusion and frustration, pressed further: "Help me understand, Mr. Angus. You refuse to escort us to the Cessnas or you do not know where to locate them? Which is it?"

"It's neither," Angus answered. "They aren't here."

"You are saying they are away on business, perhaps?"

"No, I'm saying they don't live here any longer. The Doctor cut out in Christmas of '15, went home to Chicago they say. You know, he's got a big o' house in Oak Park there, and I hear you can take a tour of it for a penny.[3] And William left a few months ago. He's in Mobile or New Orleans by now. Those two won't be back around here any time soon, I promise you."

Anna, who had been listening carefully, now jumped into the conversation: "What you say cannot be right! My husband and I have traveled by train and boat all the way from Pittsburgh and we mean to take possession of the profitable land sold to us by Dr. Cessna!"

"I can sure appreciate that, ma'am," Angus replied, briefly removing his hat as he spoke to the lady. "But there is nothing anyone can do to help you here. And, honestly, they isn't much 'profitable land' either. I fear the good Doctor sold you more swamp than profit. There have been hundreds of you folks coming down here over the last few years looking to make a fortune at the 'Santa Rosa Plantation.' But a fortune out of what? The canker worm has devoured the grapefruit and satsuma. The hurricane of 1911 blew away what was left and washed the whole island over with salt so nothing will grow now but palmetto and pine trees. And the only cattle remaining for twenty miles are grazed by General Miller and his family at Point Washington."

Andrew had a look of defeat about him as he said, "Mr. Angus, surely you are mistaken. I've seen the plat of the town – larger than Pensacola, more ambitious than New Orleans, as luxurious as Charleston – and I have written documentation from Dr. Cessna's own hand stating that the development of Santa Rosa was 75% complete!"

"Complete?" came Angus' indignant answer. "Sakes alive, it was never even begun. Oh, I

saw those same blueprints you're talking about,
5,000 acres of cosmopolitan development, but
nothing ever came of it. All this has ever been
is Hogtown Bayou – the Doctor named it after
himself after he bought all the swamp – and I
suppose it will be Hogtown Bayou once again in
a little while."

Anna interjected again: "Whatever do you
mean, sir?"

"I mean that all these folks walking around
with boards and signs are tearing down what few
buildings are left for the lumber. Even that
boat that brought you here is a repossession.
The Swain family took it from Doctor Cessna
late last year to settle a debt similar to yours,
and rumor has it that she will soon be sent up
the Mississippi. When she's gone, why, not even
the boardwalk will be left here. I'm sorry, but
the only one who's ever made a fortune at the
Santa Rosa Plantation is Dr. Charles Cessna.
Everyone else just got took for a ride."[4]

"We've been hoodwinked!" cried young Henry.

"Bamboozled!" answered his mother.

"Hornswoggled!" added Kate.

"All of the above!" Andrew finally summarized
for the family.

After a moment Angus carefully said, "Oh,
come on folks, don't take it so hard. You're
not the first to get snookered by a snake oil
salesman. You won't be the last, either. And I'm
sure, Mr. Schellman, that since you 'prospered

in dry goods,' you'll have more than enough money to get back home. Why, you might even wish to stay on a few days and take a vacation for your troubles. The Butlers have a brand new getaway over at Grayton that might suit your tastes for a week or so".

"Is it a resort?" Anna asked, briefly recovering from the shock of the conversation.

"Well, I wouldn't exactly call it that. Just a few bungalows on the beach, really," Angus answered. "But it just might be the kind of place to ease your mind of your recent troubles."

"Are there amenities there?" Andrew asked, attempting to reclaim some of his dignity. "Lawn tennis? Golf? Salons? Fine dining?"

Angus laughed heartily.

"Oh, no sir, there is nothing like that. Only a general store and a big dance hall painted as red as a beetroot. There will never be any 'amenities' at Grayton Beach or anywhere near it." Angus laughed again. "Seriously, if you think Cessna Landing is a bust, you should see it there. Nothing but gnarly oak groves and mountains of sand as white as snow: They can't give the land away. Whatever you paid Doc Cessna for your acreage here, you could have bought a hundred acres there and you would still be upside down. Blinding, desolate, silver beaches for as far as the eye can see. It's land that is absolutely useless."

"Mr. Angus, did you say, 'mountains of sand?'

Anna asked.

"Yes, ma'am."

"As far as the eye can see?" the two children inquired together.

"Endless children, endless."

"And you said it was as 'white as snow,' right?" Andrew added.

"Yes sir, as snowy white as a flock of sheep, Mr. Andrew."

With Angus' answers the Schellmans started grabbing their bags and travel trunks and began literally running back to the "Julia Belle" that had not yet pushed away from the dock.

In the midst of it all, Andrew reached to vigorously shake hands with Angus and said, "Mr. Angus, as a lifelong resident of Pittsburgh, I assure you that my family and I have no interest whatsoever in seeing or shoveling anything that resembles mountains of snow. Thank you for your kindness and keen direction on these matters. Here," Andrew stuffed his worthless deed into Angus' shirt pocket, "my Santa Rosa Plantation acreage is now yours. It appears the tract will never amount to anything anyway. I bid you a good day."

The Schellmans disappeared down the boardwalk from whence they came, re-boarding just as Captain Rogers was disembarking. Once they had pushed away from the wharf and put back into the bayou, Angus began reviewing the documents that Andrew had stuffed into his pocket. Slyly, he reached into his hip pocket and produced many more deeds exactly like the one he had just received. He was reading them all when one of his neighbors, carrying a "Diner" sign, happened by.

"Hello, William!" called the neighbor. "I expected you would be back in Chicago by now."

"As a matter of fact, I'll be heading back north soon enough," said William Cessna. "I just finished tying up a few loose ends for my brother."

"Oh, Yeah? Well, how is Doctor Cessna?" asked the neighbor.

"He is splendid, and I thank you for asking. I'll give him your regards. You know, he and I are starting a new elixir business when I get home," William said mysteriously.

"Really?" The neighbor's curiosity was obvious.

"Oh yes," Cessna answered. "It's a mail order sort of operation – thousands of bottles of $2 vitality serum delivered to people's doorsteps all around the country to aid in the 'maintenance of proper health.' We could use a good man to work as a distributor down here, a distributor who wouldn't mind getting in on the first floor."

"Well, yessiree-bob!" came the neighbor's answer. "Anything I can do to help the Cessnas – and myself, o' course."

William patted the man on the back and laughed heartily before answering.

"Truth is, we Cessnas need all the help we can get!"[5]

1   The steamship "Julia Belle" was originally named the "Charles E. Cessna," commissioned by its name sake in 1913, the founder of Cessna Landing and what would become Santa Rosa Beach, Florida. The "Belle," obtained by the Swain family, eventually became a Mississippi River steamer, but burned in December of 1931 while docked on the Monongahela River.

2   Too numerous to footnote specifically, this type of text proliferated in Northern newspapers in the early 20th century, luring investors to less than ideal Florida land developments.

3   The Dr. Charles E. Cessna House was designed and built by architect E.E. Roberts in 1905. It is now a part of the Frank Lloyd Wright Preservation Trust.

3   Cessna Landing, the original site of Santa Rosa Beach, was indeed a real estate scam in the "Florida Swampland for Sale" tradition.

4   Dr. Charles E. Cessna died in 1929 a millionaire, though most of his profits were ill-gotten. Beyond his hijinks in Walton County, Florida, he was investigated repeatedly for mail fraud and was accused by the American Medical Association of being a "loan shark, patent medicine vendor, land promoter, and scheming fraud." See Arthur J. Cramp, MD, *Nostrums and Quackery*, Volume II: *Articles on the Nostrum Evil, Quackery and Allied Matters Affecting the Public Health* (Chicago: Press of the American Medical Association, 1921), 327-330.

Blount Home
Built Circa 1800s

DAY IS DONE

The sun was falling slowly through a cloudless sky as the wind gently played in the pines, a stunning end to a beautiful summer day. On most any other evening this front porch would have been filled with family and neighbors talking about the news from DeFuniak or Boggy Bayou; singing along to

the flattop guitar now propped in the corner;
or contemplating and complaining about the
coming cotton harvest.

Indeed, the porch was crowded tonight, but
there was no gossiping or singing, and no
one paid the least bit of attention to the
lingering sunset. All eyes and conversations
were directed at the house itself where Doc
Spires was attempting to perform a miracle
behind the closed front door.'

Spires, called from his home in Gaskin
to this farmhouse in the community of Bear
Head, had gotten there as quickly as his Ford
Tudor could carry him along Highway 90.
Within minutes of arriving, he was standing
over a kitchen table that had been hurriedly
converted to an impromptu operating gurney,
bloody up to his elbows, digging what seemed
like a thousand shotgun pellets from the back
of a Walton County Sheriff's Deputy. He didn't
even know the man's name. It was no matter.
The old doctor worked as if he were trying to
save one of his own children. Out on the porch,
the somber crowd anxiously conversed as they
waited for news from within - and waited for
the family to arrive.

"This sure don't look no good..."

"Lord, I know. I ain't ever seen no doctor
ever work on a man splayed out like that, right
where he laid. Weren't no ether or nothing to
ease the man down. God help 'em both..."

"The other deputy's fairly shook up. He's a sittin' over yunder by the well house by hisself. Got Tommy's blood all over him. Thank heavens he ain't hurt none..."

"Does Sheriff Bell know about all this..."

"How did this happen..."

"I heard they was at a still over in Mossy Head when it all went to hell in a handbasket..."

Above the hushed conversation a clabbering and banging from the road could be heard. As the sound came into view, an old Model T bounded up the drive. It was Preacher Collins at the wheel, and with him was Kathryn Blount and her children. The porch emptied its contents into the yard to greet them.

Kathryn, called Katy by most folks, was a strong, determined woman near 40 years of age. She emerged from the front passenger seat of the car with a grim look on her face and a baby on her hip. Spilling out behind her was Wavine, Tommy Jr., and Alva – none of them over eight years of age. They were all barefooted and harried, undone by the news that had come to them about their father. The crowd, now pressing upon them, only intensified their misgivings, so as they popped from the car each one grabbed a handful of their mother's dress.

"Is he alive?" Kathryn asked as quickly as her feet hit the ground.

"Yes Katy, he is," someone answered, "but it shore looks bad."

Preacher Collins had made his way around to Kathryn's side of the car and took command.

"That's good news!" he more or less boomed as if addressing his congregation on Sunday morning. "But before we get too far along with the particulars, how about one of you good Christian ladies take the children for some cobbler or pie?"

Immediately three grandmothers stepped forward and gently began coaxing the Blount children to come along. Kathryn encouraged them, and after a few awkward moments the kids were off to a neighboring farmhouse where their little ears and eyes could be protected from the sights and sounds of their father's emergency surgery. Once they were out of earshot, Preacher Collins spoke again.

"Alright, can someone give Kathryn the facts of what has happened?"

At once the little crowd of vigil keepers all began speaking simultaneously. Theories. Conjecture. Rumors. Suspects. Kathryn followed the voices and faces as if she were watching a bouncing ball, trying to take it all in, but understanding none of it.

"I know what happened," came a deep voice from the back of the crowd, a voice so earnest that the folks in the crowd were silenced as quickly as they had begun. Everyone turned and there stood the deputy who had been sitting alone at the well house. Thomas Blount's blood was dried on his hands, arms, cheek, and the front of his uniform. "I know what happened," he repeated, "'cause I was there."[2]

The deputy stepped forward so as to speak to Kathryn face to face. The crowd encircled him.

"We were executing a warrant on a bunch of roughnecks from Montgomery who been causing trouble here. We caught a couple of 'em out at their 'shine shack gettin' ready to pirate another boat or break into a homestead - any sort of meanness they could get into - so we announced ourselves and told 'em to throw down any weapons they might be possessing. One of 'em froze right where he was. The other'n ran. Thomas took off after the runner while I went to shackle the other one." The deputy paused, attempting to steady his voice that had grown shaky. "But there was a third feller neither of us saw. When Thomas ran around the shack, that one popped out and drew a bead on 'im with a shotgun. Shot 'im in the back."[3]

Kathryn, for the first time, began to cry, no easy thing for a woman who had lived through the troubles of her last decade. Life wasn't easy for anyone in the Florida Panhandle in the first decades of the twentieth century, first of all, but life had been especially hard for the Blounts. Poverty; near starvation at times; the flooding that had nearly washed the county away earlier this year; she and Thomas had buried two young children.

Finally, though, it seemed things had improved. Thomas had taken this job with the Sheriff's Office, a job that would give him steady work and the family a steady paycheck. But after just two weeks on the job, just two weeks, this tragedy had struck. It was more than she and half the mourners standing in this farmyard could take. They held onto each other, heaving in sorrow, grieving with and for Kathryn.[4]

The sound of the house's front door opening drew them all from their tears for a moment. Standing there on the porch was Doc Spires. His head mirror was sitting askew his crown. His sleeves were unevenly rolled to his elbows. Great drops of sweat were dripping from his silver hair and off his chin and nose; and his clothing was soaked with sweat and blood. Wiping his hands of the stains, he stepped off the porch and into the August evening, angling directly to Kathryn.

"Are you the wife?" he asked Kathryn slowly, fatherly even.

"Yes, sir, I am," Kathryn answered, recomposed for the moment. "My name is Katy – Kathryn – you are operating on my husband Thomas Blount."

"Thomas," Doc Spires said softly. He then

took a clean handkerchief from his back pocket, removed his head mirror, and wiped his brow. "Katy," his voice more firm now, "your husband has suffered a terrible injury, as you probably know. He was shot in the back at what appears to be point blank range with a .12 gauge shotgun. He absorbed most of the shot, and I have removed all that I can get to, but there are many more pellets left in his body..."

"Doctor, tell me straight: Will he live?"

Spires glanced at the encircled crowd and then fixed his gaze on Kathryn's eyes before speaking.

"Katy, I have done all that I can do – all that anyone can do – he is in God's hands now."

There was a long, silent pause as Doc Spires stared at the top of his shoes and Preacher Collins prayerfully bowed his head. A few of the women wiped their eyes with hand sown kerchiefs while their farmer husbands held fiercely to their stoicism. Kathryn eventually spoke.

"Aren't we all, Doctor?" she asked just above the sound of her breath.

"Aren't we all, what, my dear?" Spires asked in return.

"Aren't we all in God's hands now?" she said.

The doctor reached out and put his arms around Kathryn, pulling her to his sweaty, stained shirt. "Yes ma'am," he whispered to her. "Yes ma'am, we are. Now, if you're ready, let's go visit your husband."

With his arm around her shoulder, Doc Spires led Kathryn up the steps, across the porch, and at last through the door, closing it behind them. The others remained on the steps and in the yard, but turned as one toward the door. Preacher Collins mounted the porch as if it were his pulpit.

"Good folks," he began, "I don't know what the future holds for Thomas Blount – what it holds for any of us – but I'm reminded of something the Good Lord said on his last night with his disciples. He said, 'Greater love hath no man than this, that a man lay down his life for his friends.'"[5]

A few "Amens" and a "That's right!" rang out from the gathered crowd.

"If the Lord chooses to call Tommy home, let us take some comfort in the fact that this man will go home having sacrificed himself for more than duty; but for the love of his neighbors and friends – to make this community a better and safer place."

The crowd solemnly agreed, nodding and "hallelujahing" their consent. Then, feeling the emotion of the moment, Preacher Collins turned to a young man in the crowd. Pointing to him he said, "Freddy, I know we're not at the church, but I guess church is where you make it. Would you be so kind as to play something on that guitar there for us?"

Freddy was a chorister for a few of the local churches, a simple but talented young man. He nodded, and moved to pick up the guitar propped in the corner of the porch's railing. Deliberate and unhurried he tuned the strings to his liking, and then stepped to occupy the spot at the top of the steps.

He swallowed hard and humbly said, "This is a purdy ole song from the Civil War and, well, I'd heard it my whole life but only learn't the words to it at sangin' school earlier this summer."

Freddy began to noodle about on the neck of the guitar, nervously choosing the key where he would sing. "You all've heard the tune too, I know you have, but these words, well, nobody ever seems to sang 'em. An' 'at's too bad too, cause, well, they'll break yer' heart the're so graceful."

As the sun fell below the horizon, young Freddy cleared his throat and strummed the opening chord. He closed his eyes, and opening his mouth with the voice of angel, he sang:

Day is done, gone the sun,
From the lake, from the hills, from the sky;
All is well, safely rest, God is nigh.

Fading light, dims the sight,

And a star gems the sky, gleaming bright.
From afar, drawing nigh, falls the night.

Thanks and praise, for our days,
'Neath the sun, 'neath the stars, 'neath the sky;
As we go, this we know, God is nigh.

Then goodnight, peaceful night;
Till the light of the dawn shineth bright.
God is near, do not fear, Friends, goodnight.[6]

POSTSCRIPT

Deputy Thomas G. Blount died on the kitchen table of a farmhouse in the early morning hours of August 17, 1929, having been shot the afternoon before. Because the years of the 19th and early 20th centuries were so chaotic in Walton County, Florida, record keeping was almost nonexistent. Thus, Blount's story and sacrifice – combined with his short service record – were largely forgotten. Members of his family, however, did not forget.

After years of lobbying by his family, including many who never even knew him in this life, Thomas G. Blount's service and memory were finally honored properly: His name was engraved on the National Law Enforcement Officers Memorial in Washington, DC. The family's hope is that neither he, nor any officer who has made the supreme sacrifice in the line of duty, will be forgotten, for they did not die in vain.[7]

1 "Doc Spires" in this story is Dr. William G. Spires (1885-1940) who maintained a private practice until he was nearly 80 years of age. He was the older brother, and lesser known, than Dr. Ralph B. Spires, who founded the Lakeside Clinic and Hospital in Defuniak Springs in 1939.

2 Doc Spires' appearance at Thomas Blount's surgery is hypothetical. The events herein described, however, are not. The deputy's description and the impromptu surgery on a kitchen table to save Blount's life are accurate.

3 The assailant, whose name is unknown, is said to have laughed and called out, "I shot the bastard!" when he discharged the shotgun in Thomas Blount's back. The author is indebted to Lt. Angie K. Hogeboom for this information and much of the history surrounding Thomas Blount. In addition to serving the Walton County Sheriffs Office, Lt. Hogeboom is the great-granddaughter of Thomas Blount: Lt. Angie King Hogeboom, telephone interview with author, March 12, 2015.

4 Ibid.

5 This is not only a quote from Jesus (John 15:13), this verse is engraved in Thomas Blount's gravestone in Hatcher Cemetery, Freeport, Florida.

6 Freddy's song is by Daniel Butterfield, "Butterfield's Lullaby," 1862, also known as "Day is Done." While the beautiful lyrics are obscure, the musical score is one of America's most recognized. Usually played with a bugle, it is commonly called, "Taps."

7 Ibid. Hogeboom.

WILD WILD WALTON

LET IT SHINE

"It was hot. Blisteringly hot. Nary a breeze
moved off the Bay and the sun was baking our
brains like oysters in a clay oven. We had
done our chores that morning, before the heat
came on so strong, and then tried to catch a
fish or two at the Basin. They weren't biting.

So, me and the Hobbs boys went seeking some shade in the pines. That's where we found it.

"Aubry saw it first and hollered out, 'Whooo-we, looky here boys, it's a still!' And he was right. It was a monster, too, just huge! I had never seen so much copper in one place, and to be honest, I'd never seen a working still. There were plenty of old, burned out, and rusted ones all over the woods, but this one was functioning. The barrels, coils, and worm box were all in place. This made all three of us somewhat nervous.

"Roy said, 'We's better be high-tailin' it outta here 'fore the revenuer shows up and thinks we the brewers!' But the revenuers weren't the bother, in my mind. So, I said, 'Worse yet, what if the mashman shows up and thinks we're the revenuers! They'll shoot and kill us all!' But Aubry was undeterred. 'Jack, we don't look like no revenuers,' he said, pointing to my overalls and shoeless feet. 'And there ain't no mashman to worry with, either, cause they ain't no fire. This still's a ready for the dranking.'

"I asked Aubry how he knew about such things, but he was already busying himself looking for something to drink from. He found three tin cups in the shed there, so we all three had one.

"'How 'bout a jigger fer yer dry throats?' he asked, the devil dancing in his eyes.

"'Now that you say so, it is mighty hot'n dry,' Roy answered, which only emboldened Aubry further, "I don't reckon they'd miss a thimble or two.'

'I don't want to paint myself as a righteous man. I wasn't against having a sip of white liquor, even if it was from another man's still. I just didn't want to get caught, that's all. Anyway, Roy tapped the still and drained an ounce or so into each of our cups. I stared at mine for a second or two. It wasn't quite as clear as I had been told, and it had a gamey smell about it. Meanwhile, Aubry had done chunked his sip on back and had the most terrible look on his face, sort of like a mule chewing briars. Roy was trying to get his sip down too, but looked like he did the time his mama brushed his teeth with baking powders.

"'Man, that stuff's got some twang to it,' I finally said amid the lip-smacking and sour faces.

"'I'll say! Sort of like sippin' hot tea through my pawpaw's socks,' Aubry answered. 'They must be pine needles in the top of the vat.' Then he motioned at Roy and said, 'Crawl up there and dip 'em out sos we can have a better drank.'

"Roy, as usual, did what he was told and shimmied his way to the top of that copper still, including the fire pit, a good eight feet in the air. He slipped off the top, which was already catawampus to one side, and looked in for what felt like ten minutes. I hollered at him, 'Well Roy? Is it pine needles or not?'

"'Nope, no pine needles,' he answered.

"'Magno-ya leaves, then?' Aubry asked.

"'Ain't no magnolia either!' Roy hollered back. 'It's a dead possum!'

"Well, we three commenced in the worst spitting, gagging, regurgitating, wailing, and hollering you ever seen! Roy ran all the way home and none of us saw him for a week, laid up as he was with what he claimed to be the cholera. Me, well it robbed me of the desire all together. Since that afternoon, every drop of liquor I've had to drink would fit inside a single shot glass.

"And Aubry? That's the darnedest thing, really. He grew up and became a most powerful Baptist preacher. He's never said anything about it one way or another, but I've always thought that pickled possum had a lot to do with putting the boy's mind to the Lord's work. Maybe, maybe not, but it sure did make a person think about his ways."

The deputy burst into the room as if he were a decorated G-man who was shutting down a legendary speakeasy.

"Ha!" he said, pistol drawn, "what do we have here?" And exactly what he had, was not much.

First, the deputy was a junior officer with more gumption than good sense. Second, the "speakeasy" was the dance parlor of the Santa Rosa Hotel at Cessna Landing. And third, the hardened criminals he thought to boost his career with by running them into jail, were just a few farm kids laughing, listening to the saloon piano player, and otherwise having a harmless time. These facts, however, did not dampen the officer's enthusiasm.

"I perceive this be an illegal soirée fueled by violations of our local prohibition policy," he proclaimed. "I'll be collecting your drinking cups and searching your persons to shut down the romping and the stomping fueled by your firewater."

The young revelers gave a collective groan and those with drink still in their cups quickly slung the liquid away and placed them on the table. Collectively, and simultaneously, they all placed their hands on top of their heads.

As the deputy began to pat down his "violators," Ms. Lura Cook, the owner and operator of the Santa Rosa Hotel came bursting out of the kitchen, a fire in her eyes, an apron around her narrow waist, and a rolling pin in her right hand.

"Deputy," she barked, causing the pianist to stop his playing, "does Sheriff Bell know you are down here hay-rassin' these young folk when he's said time and again to let whatever happens south of the Bay to work its ownself out? Why ain't you out stoppin' cattle rustlers or those crooks over at the landin'? Ain't no need for the law meddlin' in my business, 'specially when the Sheriff's got no knowledge of it."[2]

"Ms. Cook," the deputy answered as he continued to pat down the suspects, "I have it on good authority that there's a bootlegger in this little crowd, and I aim to run him in!"

"Horsefeathers!" came her answer. "Ever' time some new deputy gets appointed he wants to raid a bunch of stills or lock up a few young'uns to show how tough he is. Well, son, you've treed the wrong 'coon tonight. Ain't no moonshiners under my roof, I assure you."

By this point the deputy had arrived at a young woman. He reached to begin his search when she immediately, and violently, slapped him across the face. The deputy was stunned.

"You just keep yer hands to yer-self, thank ye' kine'ly!" the young lady said. "Just 'cause I'm in a dance parlor don't make me that kind of woman. Where I come from a man, badge or not, don't go a gropin' at a lady - at least not without her permission - and I have not and will not be grantin' you such."

Attempting to regain his dignity, the deputy stuttered out the question, "We-, well, well, what is your name, young lady?"

"See, there, now that's a start," she answered with a manufactured charm. "Introduce yer-self properly 'fore taking privileges that ain't yers. But my name ain't important. I just stopped in here to say 'hello' after deliverin' my daddy's smoked hams for Ms. Cook's hotel guests."

The deputy raised an eyebrow of interest.

"Hams, you say? You know, hogs love corn mash. You follow a hog through the piney woods and he'll take you right to a moonshine still."

"Boy, you duller than dishwater! They ain't no still here! And any hogs you find's done dressed, smoked, and be 'et 'fore breakfast time," the young lady answered with all the sass in the world.

"Now deputy," Ms. Cook joined in, clinching her rolling pin just a little tighter, "you've had your little look around. You can stay and shake this place down from stem to stern if you want, but you ain't gonna find no still, no corn mash, no nothing even resemblin' moonshine. I suggest you get back on your pony and light on out of here! I'd hate to have to send for Sheriff Bell just as he's sittin' down to eat his supper!"

The deputy, now feeling embarrassed and somewhat shamed, relented.

"OK, then," he said. "But I've marked every one of your faces! Don't let me catch any of you in any sort of trouble!" And with that, he was gone as quickly as he arrived.

As soon as he was out the door, everyone in the parlor turned their attention to the cheeky young woman who had defied the deputy. They watched as she reached into the pleats of her hoop skirt and produced two large mason jars of moonshine. Carefully she placed them on the table as the entire room let out a sigh of relief.

"That sho' was a close call," Ms. Cook said, scooping up the jars to take to the kitchen.

"Yes ma'am, it was," the young lady said. "It certainly was."

"Pap, is you a moonshiner?"

"Confound it, child, where'd you come up with such a question as that?"

"No wheres. But mama said you liked to drank moonshine. So, is you a moonshiner?"

"First off, bein' a moonshiner and drinkin'
moonshine is too diff'rent things. I've drank
a little white liquor from time to time, sure,
but I ain't no moonshiner. Not now."

"So," the boy said, "you was a moonshiner
and you drank moonshine. That what you sayin'?"

"Lord-a-mercy, boy, you too smart for your
own good," he said. "One day you'll probably
be going off to Tallahassee or somers like
your sister to get some serious schoolin'. My
daddy never let me finish my learnin'. I came
home from school one day, I was about your
age then, havin' learned to read and spell a
little. He looked at my book, cause he could
cipher a bit, and hollered, 'What kinda school
teaches a child to spell 'tators with a "P"!'
Next day I was home choppin' cotton for good.
But you, well, you'll make your folks and me
real proud."

"Is this your way of not answerin' my
question, Pap?"

"You just listen a minute and mind your
questions. Yes, I used to drank moonshine, more
than I should have at times. I ain't braggin',
just tellin' you 'cause you asked."

"I thought only bad people was in the
moonshine business?" the boy asked.

"Oh, they was some bad ones in the bid'ness
for sure, I swear there were. There was always
some skiffer who'd stay drunk a week and
half-dead another from his own jug; wouldn't

feed or care for his family or hit a lick at
a snake. And there were others who were just
plain greedy and mean, so caught up in the
money they'd kill anybody what got in the way,
even a lawman. But heck, son, they's greedy,
killin' people in all kinds of work who got
no respect for the law – and don't forget that
your old Pap told you so.

"For the most part, though, moonshinin' was
just a way of livin'. There weren't no pharmacies
to get medicine for the arthritis or whatever
else hurts in a man's body whose reached my
age. Couldn't help a child a stranglin' with
the cough or croop. Weren't no spirits for the
workin' people at the of the day. And folks
needed money. Homemade whiskey brought $2 a
gallon even during the Depression!"

"Wadn't that against the law, Pap?"

"Child, it was survival. This was nearly
the Moonshine Capital of the world right here
in Walton County; and not 'cause people here
liked drankin' more than other places, but
'cause people here were just 'bout starved to
death. Once the timber was all cut, the boll
weevil had eat the cotton, and the turpentine
wouldn't sell, what was folks to do?"

"I, I don't know, Pap."

"No, and all those folks didn't either, son,
so they did the best they could."

"Are there any 'shiners left in Walton
County, Pap?"

"Why, you can bet your boots they are! But the glory days have long gone. You can buy regulated liquor now, get a prescription from your doctor, and with the price of sugar and corn they ain't no money in it anyways. Besides that, the flood of '29 nearly washed every still and barrel all the way down to Cuba, and most of the moonshiners too! Boy, it was the awef'lest thang you ever seen."

"I've heard mama talk about it."

"I bet you have. Me and your granny, your mamma and daddy, and your uncle Virgil spent three days and nights on the barn roof the water got so high. Three feet of rain and the 'Hatchee was thirty feet outta her banks at Bruce and Ebro. Now, I've seen some terrible cyclones and been clobbered by some toad-choakin' rains, but that was the worst weather this country's ever seen."[3]

"And mama said she was gonna have a baby when the flood came?"

"That's right. She was carrying your sister, more than eight months along. We didn't have a bite to eat up there and the only water was what flowed 'neath the eaves of the barn. I thought your poor mama'd give birth right there on that roof. Lord, we prayed for someone to come along and help us. And the Lord answered our prayers. A couple of them ruffian moonshiners came down the river in a John Boat and plucked us like Georgia peaches right off that roof. Carried us up to Freeport where we got warm, had a meal, and where your sister was born – safe and dry. They acted a whole lot more like angels than criminals if you ask me."

"Pap?"

"What's that, my boy?"

"Has my mama ever drank moonshine?"

"Child, you've gone from preachin' to meddlin'! You'll have to ask her that question. All I'll say is that she was a child who needed doctorin' for a bad cough."

1   The Reverend Aubrey Hobbs was a Baptist minister (October 31, 1916 - December 11, 2006). His entry into the ministry via a possum in a moonshine still is complete conjecture by the author.

2   A common two-fold frustration of decades past was, 1) The citizenry south of Choctawhatchee Bay felt abandoned by law enforcement; and 2) Law enforcement did not have the means or resources to properly patrol or police south of the Bay.

3   The 1929 flood of lower Alabama and the Florida Panhandle (sometimes referred to as "The Hoover Flood") by the Choctawhatchee River remains historic in its proportions. The Florida Division of Library and Information Services has an incredible photographic collection of the event at www.floridamemory.com.

GOING HOME

Cylinders of late day sunlight were now breaking through the western windows of the boys' cottage. Looking at the clock, Celia realized she had taken much more time than she had ever intended in telling her stories. She was just standing to gather her things and tell the boys goodbye when Bobby spoke up.

"Ms. Celia, how you know 'bout all this stuff?" he asked.

"I've lived a while, that's how." she answered, returning to the edge of her seat. "And I saw a good deal of this with my own eyes, like I said, heard it with my own ears."

Bobby, the relentless interrogator that he was, continued: "But how? Was your daddy a cowboy or a lawman or somethin'?"

"That's a very perceptive observation, Bobby," Celia answered. "No, my father wasn't, but my husband was. He was Sheriff of Walton County, Florida for a time, so I got to hear and see all he heard and saw. Plus, and you boys won't believe this, but... no, I won't even tell you. You won't believe it, so I'll keep it a secret."

The boys couldn't stand this tease. They begged and squealed, pleading with Celia to tell them her mystery. Finally, having milked all the drama out of them, she relented.

"Alright, alright, I'll tell you," she began. "You won't believe it, but I was Sheriff of Walton County, Florida too!"

The boys exploded with laughter, reacting exactly as Celia had said they would. They didn't believe her. She sat there, graceful and composed, as they had their fun guffawing and pointing, rolling around on the ground like little fools. Once they settled back down, Celia pointed at Charlie and said, "Son, fetch my handbag for me from the table." He did as he was told, and, once in her hands, Celia quite deliberately reached in and produced a large, golden, five-point star. On it was inscribed the undeniable words: "Sheriff, Walton County, Florida 1938-1939."

Stunned silence filled the room. Without a word, Celia handed the heavy badge to Bobby with the instructions to examine it, and then pass it along for the others to see it as well. This took several minutes, and when the badge finally made it around the circle and back into Celia's possession, she spoke.

"You see there, boys: A lady can be a sheriff just as quick and sure as a gentleman. In all your Westerns, didn't you read about women like Annie Oakley, Calamity Jane, and Lillian Smith? These gals were better shots than most men and helped put more than one outlaw behind bars. So don't judge things so quickly, and be careful how you make light of people before you know all the facts."

Charlie, who had retrieved Celia's purse, spoke up: "Ms. Celia, did you hope on bein' a sheriff when you's was our age?" he asked.

"Lord no, child. The thought never crossed my mind," she answered. "I can't remember what I hoped on being when I was your age – but a sheriff was not on the list – I promise. Still, I was proud of having served. I did the best I could with it, though I never expected to have

ever been given the opportunity. But, that's
how life is, you see: Unexpected things happen.
You boys will see and hear such things as you
get older, why, if I could tell you about it all
right now, you wouldn't believe me – just like
you didn't believe that I was once a sheriff."

Celia smiled and readjusted in the chair.

"I suppose that's why the Good Lord only
gives us one day to live at a time. If he gave
us any more than that, I guess it would be too
much to take."

"Ms. Celia," Bobby began, "have you ever had
too much to take?"

Celia laughed out loud to Bobby's question,
such as it was, then immediately realized that
his question had been genuine. She said not a
word, at first, only looked deep into the eyes
of Bobby, Charlie, Raymond and all the little
curtain-climbing boys at her feet. Then, she
reached over and haltingly pulled the prophet
Daniel, who had been hanging there silently
all afternoon, off the flannelgraph board.

She held the little character in her hand,
looking at him for a while. He with his colorful
robe, that saintly glow, and a crooked, joyful
smile. With near reverence she stroked the
cartoon with her thumb as a single tear ran
down her cheek and splashed on Daniel's face.

"My first husband's name was Daniel, too,"
she began, "Daniel Clayton Adkinson." Celia
paused and not a single child so much as

breathed.

"My children were all at home with me that evening, just like you are with me today," she said softly. "We had eaten our supper, completed our chores, and the sun was low in the sky like it is right now. It was a Thursday. The phone rang... and... well... my Daniel never came out of that lion's den."

Celia reached into her purse and retrieved a handkerchief which she used to quickly blot the corners of her eyes. As she regained her composure, the boys remained silent, unmovable, as stunned to see this woman cry as they had been to hear she was once a sheriff.

"A few days later the governor called me and told me he was making me the sheriff of Walton County if I would take the job. It was overwhelming, I tell you. The death of my husband; faced with rearing three children, all of them your ages and younger, alone; taking an office that only one other woman had ever held in the history of the state of Florida: So yes, Bobby, there have been times when I've had more than I could take."

Bobby gave a sheepish smile and gently nodded. Raymond, meanwhile, found his feet and stepped toward the chair where Celia was sitting. Boldly, he reached into her lap and picked up the weighty sheriff's badge in his tiny little hand. Then, as if he had done so a hundred times in the past, he removed the badge from its leather bifold and gently pinned it to Celia's left lapel. He stepped back and eyed it, making sure it was straight.

"Deputies," he declared with unexpected confidence, "this is Sheriff Celia Adkinson!" And with that, he snapped a smart salute as if Old Glory herself had been raised. Every child in the room stood and saluted. Some grinning, some still shocked that their sweet, little Bible teacher was a "woman of the law," and some were suddenly emotional, including Charlie, whose cheeks now dripped with tears.

At that moment the command, "Ten-Hut!" was heard in the back of the room. Celia raised her head to look, and all the boys turned as well. Mr. Weaver was there, his face beaming, and he had the older boys of the ranch with him. In unison they had joined the younger boys in saluting Sheriff Adkinson. Apparently they had slipped in quietly and had heard a number of the stories she had been telling. It was a magical moment, nothing short of something sacred.

"Now that's enough!" Celia finally said, a brilliant smile cutting through her red, embarrassed cheeks. "Stop saluting! And that's an order!" she commanded.

The boys burst into laughter, a sweet release of so much emotion, and even Mr. Weaver's presence wasn't enough to keep them from bounding all about the room. He attempted to

rein them in for supper, with the older boys'
help, and Celia, with her heart full, began to
gather her things and take them to the car for
the ride home.

On her second or third trip to the car with
arms full of bags, flannel boards, and empty
dishes, she was joined by Mr. Weaver.

"Ms. Celia," he began, "I'd be happy to call
Live Oak and book you an overnight room there
so as to avoid that long drive this late and
all. You'd be welcome to stay here, of course,
but they ain't an open bunk anywheres, not
even in me and my wife's home. They're boys
stacked in like cordwood, ever'where."

"That is terribly kind, Mr. Weaver, and I
thank you," Celia answered. "But that won't be
necessary. However, please make use of that
telephone to call my husband so he will not
worry. If you don't mind the long distance,
toll, that is."

"Oh, yes ma'am, of course," Weaver answered.

"That'll be no problem." His hands pushed
deep into his pockets, Mr. Weaver tumbled a
few stones over with his wingtips and studied
the ground as Celia sorted her things in the
trunk of the Chevrolet. Finished, she closed
the latch and turned to Mr. Weaver.

"Harry," she said quite forcefully, "I've
lived and worked in a man's world my whole
life. Your species is not the most subtle. You
have something to say, so, out with it."

Mr. Weaver yanked his hands from his pockets and placed them on his hips, a hangdog look on his face, resembling one the cottage boys rather than the ranch's director.

"Ain't nothin' Ms. Celia. I was just about to say somethin' about that long ride home and how it'd be dangerous and why no woman should try such a thing and all that. But my ears cut off my tongue. After all you'd said in there to them boys, well, I reckon they ain't much you're scared of. So, without my usual speech to give, I was just sort of standin' here knock-kneed."

Celia chuckled, taking Mr. Weaver's awkwardness as a compliment, and opened the door to her car before speaking.

"Mr. Weaver, I don't know much about life or anything else for that matter. I just know we are here, here in this world for a spell, subject to all manner of beautiful and terrible things. But through it all, we can't be afraid. We only do the best we can with what life gives us and trust the Good Lord to take care of the rest."

Celia smiled again, gave the giant badge still ensconced on her left lapel a quick shine, then extended her hand.

"I'll see you next time, Mr. Weaver," she said. "I'm going home."

With those words, she climbed behind the wheel of that Chevrolet and pointed it west toward the setting sun. Toward Walton County. Toward Wild, Wild Walton.

1   These words are inspired by the memorable quote of
    Frederick Buechner: "Here is the world. Beautiful and
    terrible things will happen. Don't be afraid." Frederick
    Buechner, Beyond Words: *Daily Readings in the ABC's
    of Faith* (New York: HarperCollins, 2004), 139.

Dedication of the Sid M. Saunders Memorial Cottage by his family - Live Oak, Florida

Small "cracker-style" homesite around the turn-of-the-century in South Walton County.

The 1929 flood of lower Alabama and the Florida Panhandle (sometimes referred to as "The Hoover Flood")

Masonic Hall and General Merchandise store buildings, not far from the "Fifty Cent" Murder site in Freeport.

135

ABOUT THE AUTHOR

Scientists say that the beautiful, sugar-white beaches of the Florida Panhandle are the result of erosion from the Appalachian Mountains. A sand dune that we enjoy today, as we are told, was once a mountain top in Georgia, but over time that mountain washed all the way down to the sea. There's no better description for writer, Ronnie McBrayer.

Before making his home near the beautiful beaches of Walton County, Florida more than a decade ago, Ronnie was a life-long Georgian, born and raised in the foothills of the Appalachian Mountains. Today, having washed down to the sea, he is the author of multiple books and publications, a talented musician, a local pastor, and a nationally read columnist. His weekly feature, "Keeping the Faith," is syndicated in more than 75 print and online outlets with a circulation of six million readers. Ronnie's next book, "Grayton Beach: A History" will be released in 2016.

Ronnie maintains a contagious faith, a cheerful schoolboy wit, and an applauded storytelling style that invites his readers and listeners to discover new ways to experience personal freedom and grace. With his wife Cindy – a talented artist in her own right – and his three sons, Ronnie might be a long way from home, but he is never far from his roots. Visit his website at www.ronniemcbrayer.net.

Made in the USA
Middletown, DE
16 April 2017